MW01627729

BrandsFormation®

BrandsFormation®

HOW TO TRANSFORM YOUR GOOD HEALTHCARE PRACTICE INTO A GREAT LOCAL BRAND

Chuck Mefford
with Lori M. Lovett

Published 2010

ISBN 978-0-9815850-1-7

Visit our website at www.brandsformation.com

I dedicate this book to Roann, the love of my life.

*From the moment we met, I knew it was you
that I wanted to spend the rest of my life with.*

The best is yet to come!

Chuck

Acknowledgments

"The star of the team is the team"

– John Wooden, Legendary Basketball Coach
October 14, 1910 – June 4, 2010

I'd like to publicly thank "my team" for your contributions to this book and for furthering the BrandsFormation® brand.

In alphabetical order:
Greg Jessen
Jeffrey Schmidt
Brandon Vincent
and
Dr. Susan Badaracco
Brian Borchardt PT, MPT
Dr. Bryan Borgfeld
Dr. Thomas A. Brooks
Dr. Randy Butler
Dr. Lawrence Cairns and Mrs. Susan Cairns
Dr. Terry Cowgill
Dr. Karl Foster
Dr. John Gomez
Dr. Gustov Lo
Dr. Shane Mason
Dr. David Olive
Steven Olson BS, OTR/L
Janette Venaas-Gilbraith, MS, CCC-SLP

Foreword

The man who arguably holds the title of the wisest king, Solomon, penned, "A good name is more desirable than great riches; to be esteemed better than silver or gold." (Proverbs 22:1 NIV)

Not that Solomon decried wealth – he was probably the richest king of the ancient world. But he knew that at the end of the day, integrity, name recognition, esteem – ***branding*** if you will, was far more important.

For centuries, medical practitioners have been held (or have held themselves) to codes of high integrity and have sought to distance themselves from any appearance of charlatanism common in traveling faux-medical snake-oil vendors who hawk their potions with glitzy ads and loud sideshows. In the early 20th Century, credentialed practitioners were restricted from advertising in Great Britain while the same was frowned upon by the American medical establishment.

When I finished my training in Obstetrics and Gynecology in the mid-70's, advertising was considered "unprofessional" – certainly not a mark of integrity. Everyone, so it was thought, knew what to expect of a physician and viewed each one as cut from the same cloth. Practices were built purely by word of mouth referrals or good ol' boy networks of fraternity brothers. The physician's *specialty* was his or her "brand" with standard expectations of available services.

This tradition resulted in inertia in medical practice, slow advancement and few entrepreneurs. The code was, "we've never done it that way before."

My branding story began when I decided to drop Obstetrics after delivering several thousand babies with the hope of bringing increased regularity to my nighttime sleep and family involvement. I resigned from a large multispecialty clinic and established a solo Gynecology-only practice in the same community. I agreed to not actively recruit my former patients even though there was not a no-compete clause. We sought effective ways to attract patients. We put a few dollars in several different media outlets but really didn't see many results from print ads, community TV weather "crawls" or sporadic spots on the radio.

Our lives changed when we were invited to attend a half-day BrandsFormation® seminar led by Chuck Mefford at a local college. That life changing day in February, 2007 almost wasn't! Our corner of Southwest Michigan was blanketed by eighteen inches of heavy, wet snow overnight. All schools were closed and community events cancelled. My wife Susan and I listened to the local closings on radio and ventured out to hear Chuck hoping the BrandsFormation® seminar was still on.

We were welcomed by other hardy souls who had braved the elements to improve their own branding process – people in food industries, communications, hospitality and even hospice. I don't recall another physician being in the audience.

We were so impressed with the potential of what we were learning that when we had the opportunity for a one-on-one appointment with Chuck, we made sure to be at the front of the line. We wanted to position our practice, *Femme Vitale Gynecology*, at the top of the branding ladder. We wanted our practice to become a household name in our market; one that every woman would think of when she needed gynecologic care. We wanted to demonstrate compassionate care, partnering with every woman to help her "dance over the hurdles of life" with robust vitality. We hoped that our comprehensive gynecologic care with a natural twist would be so comforting that women wouldn't even notice the high tech aspects.

With Chuck's help, and the expertise of a local radio station staff, we were able to birth a coherent branding strategy that has garnered recognition in our market. Chuck Mefford created some remarkable strategies to take the old word-of-mouth paradigm and expand it, increment by increment, with a consistent, oft-repeated message in an unforgettable emotional anchor.

I know there were a few raised eyebrows in the medical community when we started advertising – especially since we're a gynecological practice. We stayed the course of integrity and appropriateness with guidance from our local radio team. Honestly, we have had only one negative comment but hundreds of positive responses. Our appointment schedule is filled by women who came because of the *Femme Vitale Gynecology* ads heard on our local stations. In fact, within 18 months of our BrandsFormation® launch, our new patient business increased 53%! Today, there are several more medical practices in our area enhancing their position and brand awareness. We welcome their camaraderie and enthusiasm.

Patients no longer want cookie-cutter practitioners. If yours is a healthcare practice that has unique services, expertise or procedures anchored in values that are meaningful to today's generation, or if your caring, compassion and personal dedication to your patients is your focus, we can enthusiastically recommend that you read and implement what this book has to teach you. You will have no regrets. People want medical marketing with integrity and verifiable claims. Your decision to follow the BrandsFormation® system will lend credibility to your "good name" and enhance your bottom line.

Dr. Larry Cairns
www.femmevitale.net

Contents

Introduction

Mayo Clinic. Okay … just Mayo. That's all you have to say and almost everyone with a pulse has heard of it. Most can't tell you where it's located but that's not what's important to them. They just know that if they ever find themselves in a puzzling or critical medical situation, there's no better place to seek healthcare. Every industry has a gold standard. Rolex, Mercedes, Ritz-Carlton … and in healthcare … it's Mayo.

Numerous books have been written about the Mayo Clinic and how they have achieved such recognition and respect. There are countless branding lessons to be learned from Mayo, not only for healthcare categories, but for any industry.

Mayo has achieved gold standard status by having a laser focus on patient care and attending to even the smallest of details. The book *Management Lessons from Mayo Clinic* outlines the many ways the organization demonstrates care for their patients realizing that "no one wants to go to a hospital." The most thoughtful and mind-blowing example I read was regarding the selection of marble for their buildings. "A Mayo Clinic facilities team travels to the marble quarries to scrutinize the marble blocks for the slabs on the walls or floor to ensure that no potentially disquieting images of human forms or diseases are suggested by the natural designs in the stone." They are even attending to minutia that patients wouldn't consciously be aware of. That's certainly going the distance in patient care.

At this stage in their development, the Mayo Clinic could most likely forego what some might consider window dressing or extras, but to them, it's part of their DNA ... it's who they are and who people have come to expect them to be. The folks at Mayo get it. They aren't just known for patient care, they eat, sleep and breathe it. Over time, the truth of that brand has settled on the minds of people all over the world. What would it take for your practice to be branded the "Mayo way" in your local market? What would you have to do to be the healthcare practice patients think of first whenever they need your service?

BrandsFormation® is your answer. I know your time is precious and reading a book on anything but the latest findings and technologies in your area of specialty might seem out of the question. If you will invest your time learning about my system I promise the payoff will be well worth it. Whether you are a dentist, doctor, weight loss specialist, veterinarian or you perform laser skin care, this book will teach you what you never learned in school about marketing your practice.

Are you great at what you do? Do you have something special to offer that others in your field of practice aren't delivering? That's great! Your mother is undoubtedly very proud of you! But if nobody knows this but you (and your mom) what's the point?

This book is not about how to become a better doctor or healthcare provider. You can be the best there is in your city, your state, or heck ... all the world! While your expertise is an essential component for the success of your practice, this alone will not guarantee your full growth potential.

This book is about helping you become a better business person and growing your practice.

You may not think of yourself as a business owner, but that's what you are. Your patients may not acknowledge that you run a business, but you do.

I know many doctors even complain that they have a hard time getting patients to pay for their services and say they are treated as though they are part of some kind of entitlement program. People wouldn't dream of withholding payment at the time service is rendered in any other industry. They sure wouldn't walk out of a grocery store with items in hand and skip past the check out. That's called stealing. Nonetheless, you are running a business and to do so effectively, you need to be equipped with some marketing tools that nobody bothered to give you in school.

You've got a story to tell, but you just don't know how to tell it.

That's where my system comes in. I've helped discover and tell the stories of hundreds of businesses and healthcare providers and, in so doing, have helped them carve out a place in their market that has dramatically elevated their business. Like them, you have a story to tell. This book will help you discover and polish that story and ultimately grow your already good practice into a great local brand.

Now let me say, if your practice is on life support, this won't get you out of bed and running a 10K anytime soon, if ever. If this is the case, you need to go immediately to the back of this book and take an honest look at our TouchPoints

360° Checklist. This is where you will find specific tools to hone your attention to what skews patient perspective, both positively or negatively. In essence, here is where you can give your practice a check-up. My BrandsFormation® system is all about accelerated word of mouth, therefore, I don't think you want help telling your story until you have given your practice a clean bill of health.

On the other hand, if you are operating a healthy practice, the reason you still have vacancies in your appointment book is not your fault. In spite of the incredible hours of classes, labs, internships and rotations required to earn your degree, you were never taught in school a thing about how to grow your business. Don't spend too much time beating yourself up. You've finally figured out you need help, and you've come to the right place to get it. By implementing BrandsFormation®, you can be the healthcare practice people think of first when they need your type of service.

Imagine being free to do what you got into medicine to do – actually focus on helping and healing. In this book, you will learn how to edge past your competition and you will gain the tools to confidently and systematically market your practice for long-term success. As you will see, healthcare professionals and other business owners have put BrandsFormation® to work and have found that they have reaped a better return on their time investment than by any other means they've tried before.

This is a step-by-step playbook with many elements that can be delegated to office managers and other staff members. This will also help prevent you from being bogged down with the perfunctory but vital details needed to successfully brand and manage your practice. You can reinvent the wheel. You can continue the trial and error methods that have left you frustrated. OR...you can follow a simple and proven system.

Still not convinced you need BrandsFormation®? Let's think about the countless changes that have occurred in healthcare in the past few years. This is not your father's healthcare system:

- Insurance reform that scarcely anyone can keep up with
- Patients who self-diagnose through search engines
- People are hungry for information. TV has evolved from fictional doctors like Marcus Welby, MD and Quincy, to real life, reliable experts such as Dr. Sanjay Gupta and Dr. Oz
- Healthcare reform which, at present, can't be measured insofar as how it will affect private practice, insurance companies and patients
- Pharmaceutical companies with advertising budgets that could choke a horse, leading to more conflicting information for your patients
- Social media/networking sites
- Market growth
- Cafeteria style benefits packages allowing patients more choices in healthcare providers
- Big-box retailers, supermarkets and pharmacies offering basic healthcare tests, shots and screenings
- Media reports abounding in conflicting medical news

Obviously, your plate is quite full in the "changes department" and I know you're not looking for more bad news, but all of these things are completely out of your control. What the government does with healthcare is out of your control. How businesses provide benefits for their employees is out of your control. What you can control, however, is whether people consider your practice first when they have a need you can meet.

As we proceed through this book you will learn how to:

- be the healthcare practice people think of first whenever they need your service
- get a solid return on investment from your advertising
- craft an E-Speech
- tell your great story (brand your practice)
- extend your brand throughout your practice
- implement a solid strategy for long-term growth and success
- avoid the three most common mistakes in marketing

BrandsFormation® will simplify and maximize your marketing efforts and bring about accelerated growth to your practice. The same marketing strategies that have rocketed big name businesses into iconic status are successful because fundamentally, they are good in principle. These strategies are also working for fertility clinics, veterinarians, laser treatment centers and heart surgeons, to name a few. What teams of marketing professionals and big time advertising agencies on Madison Avenue do to drive home a message on behalf of Nike or Starbucks, you can duplicate on a smaller scale and reap the benefits.

As the saying goes, "it's not brain surgery."

1

What is Branding?

(And Do You Need It?)

Undoubtedly, you have a wall where you proudly display your hard earned degrees. After years without sleep or decent food and having spent an ungodly amount of money for your education, you certainly deserve the recognition. However, let me assure you, as important as your degrees are to you, your credentials don't mean "jack squat" to your patients. Very few people (in fact, none that I know) take the time to research your education, verify your standing with the medical board, or even check your certification. Why is this? Because patients are consumers and they're shopping for more than a healthcare provider with some nicely framed degrees. Everything a consumer/patient is looking for can be found in this little fill-in-the-blank exercise. If you answer correctly, you move to the head of the class.

People do not buy products or services.
People buy what products or services ___________________.

People buy what products or services DO FOR THEM! Think about it…would you rather buy:

- *A mattress … or … A good night's sleep?*
- *A hospital stay … or … Wellness?*
- *A camera … or … A captured memory?*
- *A dental appointment … or … A great smile?*
- *A chiropractic adjustment … or … Relief from pain?*
- *Physical therapy … or … The ability to love, laugh and live life to its fullest?*

The answers are pretty obvious. People always go for the benefit offered by a product or service. Start thinking in terms of what benefit you offer your patients. This will be the "theme" of your story.

How impactful can successful branding be? You tell me …

Like a good neighbor ________________

The real thing ________________

Finger-lickin' good ________________

Give us 15 minutes ________________

We'll leave the light on for you ________________

I'm Lovin' It! ________________

Good to the last drop ________________

You probably had no trouble knowing exactly which companies own each of these phrases. That's because these companies successfully branded their names and have claimed "mental real estate" in the minds of consumers. Very simply put,

BRANDING is being the first business people think of when they need your type of product or service.

Who understands this best?
The big guys do!

- Will you "live better" because you shop at WalMart?
- Will you become a "champion" by eating Wheaties?
- Is Coca-Cola truly "the real thing?"

It doesn't matter. Each of these companies have branded themselves in the minds of consumers by making the all important emotional connection with them. Branding your practice will help you do the same in your local market.

Consumers (your prospective patients) are looking for their very best choice when they need your type of healthcare. Convincing them that you are that best choice will take time and effort, but it can be done, so keep plugging away with me. The good news is, you have a leg up on most other business owners. In the field of healthcare, your prospects are automatically going to have an emotional response to your practice because they are embarking on a trust and needs-based journey with you.

The consumer relationship in each healthcare experience is so much more personal than other consumer relationships. In almost every case, patients walk into a healthcare facility with a problem, concern or dissatisfaction of some kind. The emotional element is automatic. It's there whether you acknowledge it or ignore it. But you ignore it at your own peril.

Think about it ... how hard would it be to get someone to make an emotional connection to a set of new tires or a breakfast cereal? Even so, look at Michelin & Wheaties. Michelin pulled off the masterful ad campaign showing a baby happily rotating inside one of their tires. Their words resonated with all parents when they said "Because so much is riding on your tires." Notice, they really didn't talk about their tires. Without listing the many features of their great brand of tires, they let consumers know that Michelin tires were the tires to buy if you cared at all about your loved ones.

All Wheaties had to do to make an emotional connection is to label themselves "The breakfast of champions." Again, no mention of the cereal itself. The hook is in what the cereal can do for you...make you a champion too! Tires and breakfast cereals are just daily consumables. They don't really require much distinction between brands for a desirable outcome to occur. One fills your belly for breakfast, the other keeps your car moving down the road ... but the way they've been branded sure leaves us believing that their specific products will do something special for us.

Your service is already seen as a need before your consumer comes looking for you, so the opportunity to imprint a positive emotional message to your prospects is like a bird in hand. With branding, your practice can more easily stand out among all the cluttered messages about consumable products and less essential services.

Branding is not a slogan, a logo or a slick tagline ... it is defining what makes you different ... what makes you better than your competition.

Branding is a gut feeling ... an idea about your practice ... about what makes you the prospective patient's very best choice. Now to get to that gut feeling, you have to think about your answer to the following questions: "Who are you, and why should I do business with you?" How you answer this will largely determine your success at branding your practice.

The most important thing to remember before you respond to that question is that your answer needs to be **benefit focused**. This will require you hanging up your doctor hat for a bit and taking on the perspective of your patients and prospects. What you are really answering is what your care or service will do for the patient. Your answer to this question will become your **Elevator Speech** ... and I will teach you how to craft one so that you can own mental real estate in the minds of your prospects.

Is <u>BRANDING</u> really necessary for healthcare practices?

Well, you decide ... BrandsFormation® is truly only useful if you want to:

- Grow your profits
- Attract better patients & cases
- Enhance your reputation in your market
- Differentiate yourself from your competition

If your profits are not blowing your mind, you're not well-known in your community, you're swimming in a sea of competitors or you're fresh out of school, you absolutely need to brand your practice.

I don't have to tell you how important word of mouth is to the success of your practice and to your reputation. In today's world of social media, blogging and Internet loops, your prospects are just a few keystrokes away from finding out who all of their contacts think is the best veterinarian ... best chiropractor ... best plastic surgeon ... best weight loss center ... and the list goes on.

Will what others say about you (word of mouth)
be controlled by you
... or it will be controlled by others?

Branding helps put you in the driver's seat so that what is said about you is created and controlled by you. You create the words based on the values and benefits you want to communicate to your patients. The moment a patient has made initial contact with your office is when their word of mouth story begins to be formulated. Even someone who has only gotten as far as the appointment stage will have something to say about your practice if the opportunity presents itself. No matter how well the values of your practice are being executed, you cannot control or even know what that patient will say about you. BrandsFormation® teaches you how to drive the branding process and control what prospects and patients come to think and feel about you.

WHERE DO YOU BEGIN?

Remember how I talked about storytelling? This is the defining moment for your story. Think about what makes you different, special, better ... it may be your bedside manner, the amount of time you give to each patient, how well your entire office interacts with every patient that comes through your door. This goes beyond any specialty you studied. I'm not talking about your credentials, your updated technology or your peer reputation. I'm talking about connecting with people on the deepest level...the emotional level.

FIND SOMETHING YOU DO WELL AND BUILD YOUR REPUTATION AROUND IT

In healthcare, branding is about the relationship that your patients have with you and your entire staff. It is about the expectations that you've set through your message and what benefit they will receive from experiencing your service. By uncovering your uniqueness ... your positive difference, you are identifying your **Difference Maker**.

See if you can find the Difference Maker in the following true story:

A mother of a six-year-old girl learns that her daughter needs a tonsillectomy. Although this is a routine procedure, no surgery is minor when it's being performed on one of your children. On recommendations, the mother makes appointments with two different doctors. Upon the visit to Doctor #1, mom is impressed that the practice is located on site of one of the best hospitals in her metropolitan city. This surely proves the doctor is qualified. The waiting room is full ... hmm ... "He must be really well respected," thinks the mom. The receptionist is pleasant enough, décor well-appointed, environment seems clean. So far, so good ... Then comes the true first impression! In walks a well-dressed man looking to be in his mid-50's. He's clearly experienced. Doctor #1 quickly introduces himself to the mother. As he flips through the patient chart, the mother takes notice of his customized running shoes with his name embossed on the side. He agrees the surgery is necessary and leaves mom with a video to watch which explains the procedure. The doctor prepares to leave the room and he assures the mother that his nurse will be in momentarily to discuss any questions she may have. For some reason, the mother is uneasy. Everything seemed to be going fine until the doctor entered the room. Video in hand, the mother leaves the office saying she'll call to schedule the surgery at another time, and promptly makes an appointment to see Doctor #2.

Fast forward to the next appointment: Doctor #2 offices in a modest stand-alone building along the access road of a new tollway. His waiting room is empty, his receptionist polite but aloof. Mom is now thinking Doctor #1 is looking pretty good. When a very young Doctor #2 enters the examining room, he goes right past mom and immediately introduces himself to the little six-year-old girl. He discusses the options, timeline, procedure and asks the daughter what questions she has. The tonsillectomy is scheduled before the mom leaves the office of Doctor #2.

Doctor #2 carried the day ... so what was his Difference Maker? To the mother in this story ... it was that this doctor realized the child wasn't "just another case," the child was her daughter! The way Doctor #2 treated the daughter trumped any advantage Doctor #1 might have had based on his standing in the medical community, years of experience or affiliation with a major medical center.

Doctor #1 doesn't need to brand his practice ... his

waiting room is full (for now.) Doctor #2 however, needs to brand his practice because he has a compelling Difference Maker and that is crucial to unlocking his growth potential. Doctor #2 might word his DM this way: "understanding that your child is your most precious treasure" ... or ... "caring for your child as much as you do" ... or ... "your child's health matters most".

Have the courage to offend your competition! Ideally, your branding will be unique; not all things to all people. Don't be surprised when your competition attacks your claims or tries to copy what you're doing. That's just confirmation that your branding is working.

Additionally, some patients will not want what you have to offer. That's okay. Trying to be all things to all people will make you common and forgettable...that doesn't get you in the game.

When considering your Difference Maker, think about:

- What makes you unique?
- What makes you memorable?
- What benefit will your patients receive each time they visit?
- What kind of promise can you make....and keep?
- What competitor, if any, can say the same thing?

Make notes, ask friends and family for their perspective and be willing to honestly evaluate what differentiates you from your competition.

Having a Difference Maker is life or death here. You had better have a strong DM or decide to become the lowest priced healthcare provider in your category. But be forewarned ... being known as the low cost practice certainly won't lead to a great reputation, better patients and better cases or profit growth. The best you can hope for in this case is mediocrity and an ever-changing list of unconvinced, uncommitted patients.

On the other hand, if you effectively brand your healthcare practice, not only will you be rewarded with new patients and loyalty from existing patients ... you will also experience something we all need and rarely get:

Forgiveness Insurance

That's right ... if you brand your practice by setting yourself apart and being who you say you are, your patients will much more readily accept and forgive a mistake here and there. If you're a lover of Coca-Cola, you will easily understand what I mean. If you purchase a bottle of Coke that happens to lack that great "burn your throat" fizz we have all come to love, because of your loyalty to the brand you will not jump ship and change colas. Whereas, if you purchased another brand that is not your normal favorite and it's flat, you will most likely never return to this brand. If consumers aren't loyal to a brand, whether it's a soft drink or a doctor's office, they won't readily forgive even the smallest of mistakes. Through branding, and becoming the healthcare practice that people think of first and feel best about, you will benefit from forgiveness insurance.

BRANDSFOR℞MATION
Branding Prescription:

- *Branding is: being the healthcare practice people think of first when they need the service you provide.*

- *People don't buy products or services. People buy what products and services do for them.*

- *To get started, answer these two questions:*
  Who are you?
  Why should I do business with you?

- *Your response needs to be benefit (or patient) focused. Look at your practice through the eyes of your patients.*

www.brandsformation.com

2

Being First

(It Worked for Columbus)

First matters! Even from childhood, we understand what it means to be first. We want to be first in line, first chosen for the team, first to raise our hand in class. As we grow up, first still matters. Our first crush, first car, first kiss, first date, first job … firsts evoke memories and feelings. What makes first special? Think back on your first love. Even if it ended badly, you have to smile just thinking about it. It's memorable because you had not ever experienced it before. *Firsts* come with emotional connections.

You don't have to be a marketing genius to be first. You just to have to adopt the Nike way of thinking … *JUST DO IT!* Ever hear of the "egg of Columbus"? The expression refers to a popular story of how Christopher Columbus was challenged by critics after discovering the Americas. They were claiming that this was really no great accomplishment and, that in a country like Spain abundant with great and knowledgeable men, many could have experienced the same discovery on such an adventure. Instead of responding to the comments, Columbus asked for a whole egg to be brought to him. Upon receipt of the egg, he challenged the men present to make the egg stand on its end. All tried, and all were unsuccessful. Columbus took his turn and gently tapped the egg on the table, breaking it slightly. With this, the egg stood on its end. The confounded men exclaimed, "anyone could have done that." "Yes," said Columbus, "anyone could have, but only I did!" Once a challenge has been accomplished, many could copy it. But someone has to be **first!**

Think about being first in terms of marketing. Getting into the consumer's mind with a new idea, product or service trumps coming behind and trying to convince that consumer you've got something "better."

Being first is not necessarily about getting to the marketplace FIRST with your service or product, but about getting into the minds of consumers FIRST.

At its core, branding is about being the healthcare practice that people think of first when they need your product or service. Being first can make you top dog! Take FedEx for example. They were the first at overnight delivery. Now everyone says they are "FedEx'ing" a package even if they are using a generic sender. Hertz was the first rental car company on the scene and now all they have to say is "Hertz #1" and therefore, they are. Other firsts to own their category are Polaroid, Xerox, Hewlett Packard, Kleenex and Band-Aid to name a few. They have each become generic because they created the category. **First** is measurable and something that can be agreed upon, whereas best is based on a variable system of measurement.

Papa John's Pizza wedged their way into the crowded delivery pizza category with *better tasting pizza* but they followed through and validated that claim with better ingredients. *Best* can be really great … just much harder to prove than *first*!

Now, you're probably thinking, "How does this help me? Unless I'm willing to move to East Cactus, Utah and perform surgeries on left-handed dwarves with brain tumors, there are no first place spots available." True. However, there's hope. To understand how to be first, short of having a Louis Pasteur level discovery, we first have to examine how the mind works and what it does with product and service categories in the marketplace.

This is where the pioneering work of Jack Trout has turned the world of marketing upside down. To those of you who are not familiar with Jack Trout, he is considered "the father of positioning." He has worked with Papa John's, Southwest Airlines, IBM and Wells Fargo, among others.

The 1981 book by Trout and his partner Al Ries, *Positioning: The Battle for Your Mind*, asserts these points about the human mind:

- Minds are **limited** – they can only remember a small number of units
- Minds **hate confusion** – they are attracted to simplicity and order
- Minds are **insecure** – which is why they are easily swayed by convincing authority
- Minds **rarely change** – and because they find changes so difficult, much of our intelligence is devoted to rationalization, that is, coming up with rational explanations for our emotional decisions
- Minds can **lose focus** – they are easily distracted and confused by vague communication or images

These factors all point to one solution: simplicity!

Communicate with simplicity and your Difference Maker will stand out and set you apart from your competition. Attaching a key word or phrase to your practice can do for you what the word "safety" has done for Volvo, or what the words "good neighbor" have done for State Farm, or what the words "Life is Good" have done for an independent t-shirt company in Boston. Implementing my system will help you to control not only what is *said* about you, but even what is *thought* about you.

As "Exhibit A" consider Terry Cowgill, DDS. He was one of many dentists in his Midwest market. He didn't want to just be another dentist whose *Yellow Page* ad lined the kitty litter box. And he didn't want his practice to look, smell or feel like a dental office. He realized that nobody wants to be drilled and filled, but everybody wants a great smile. So, Dr. Cowgill became the first dentist in his market to "keep you smiling." Through the use of humor and Dr. Cowgill's willingness to be a little animated, he has implemented a strategy that causes people to "smile" when they think of him. Surely there are dentists in his same zip code who also care about their patients' smiles, or who can crack a joke as well as Dr. Cowgill, but they didn't get to the marketplace first with this idea … he did.

Consequently, he's stuffed to the rafters with patients and only has to maintain his first place status. He doesn't have to convince anyone he's better, because he was first and therefore the perceived market leader. Was this a complex marketing strategy? No, simplicity is key.

UNDERSTANDING LADDERS IN THE MARKETPLACE

Here's a test:

- How many brands of ***toothpaste*** can you name?
- How many ***rental car*** companies can you name?
- How about ***pain relievers***?
- Or ... ***body wash***?

How did you do? If you truly shot from the hip and didn't get help from Google, then, you, like most people didn't name more than seven brands per category. Amazingly, I've been able to count roughly 37 brands of toothpaste, 14 rental car companies, 19 brands of pain relievers and over 100 brands of body washes available to the American consumer.

You are a rare individual if you were able to name more than seven items in each category. Most people are limited to between four or five.

Each category (whether a product or a service) has a mental ladder on which consumers subconsciously rank the top brands. These top brands have captured mindshare on the first few rungs of the ladder, leaving the rest to wander aimlessly among a herd of unknowns. Harvard psychologist George A. Miller conducted research on how many units of thought the average mind can retain. He concluded that seven is the maximum number for most individuals. Hearing of this, a minister friend of mine responded, "That's right. Even regular churchgoers usually can't remember all of the Ten Commandments. If challenged to name them, they usually peter out after about six."

So, what does this mean to you as a healthcare

professional? If you're not on one of the top three rungs, you won't even be considered when prospective patients are deciding where to go for the service you offer. You simply MUST develop and implement a strategy to get on that mental ladder in one of the top three positions. The top three, in any business category get the phone calls, the appointments ... and the profits!

MATURE VERSUS OPEN LADDERS

A Mature (or saturated) Ladder is one where most consumers can readily name businesses or products for up to seven rungs. Banks are a great example of this. In a recent study in a Midwest market, all but nine percent of people surveyed could readily name a bank, and most could name several. That means mindshare has already been captured by the top three rung holders, and a new bank would have to find a way to wedge itself onto that ladder by creating a new sub-category.

To get an idea of what I mean, try this exercise. Fill in as many rungs on the following ladder with bank names as you can:

____

____

____

____

____

____

____

____

____

How did you do? Now try the same thing, but this time name as many podiatrists as you can:

____

____

____

____

____

You may notice that I didn't give you as many rungs on the ladder for podiatrists. It's partially because I don't want to frustrate you and partially because I'm a bit of a tree hugger and just couldn't stand to waste the paper. After all, you're lucky if you can name even one podiatrist (and recalling people from school with a specialty in podiatry doesn't count!)

An Open Ladder exists when there is a category in which consumers are hard-pressed to name multiple businesses or products, and often fail to name any at all… like the podiatrist ladder. This is typically because the category has not traditionally advertised. For example, in that same study that showed the saturated bank ladder, 71% of people surveyed could not name a chiropractor and 52% couldn't name a dentist…not a single one. Kind of makes you wonder about their dental health, doesn't it? Most service oriented businesses fall into the Open Ladder category because people don't give the category a thought until they have a pressing need. This is really good news for anyone in the healthcare industry, but believe me, it won't be for long. As the competition grows and savvy healthcare professionals fight for their spot on a ladder, the rungs will quickly fill up.

Open Ladders are the keys to the kingdom. You've just

been given a map to where the treasure lies. There are many Open Ladders left in healthcare, which means the field is wide open to whoever gets there "firstest with the mostest." The first on an Open Ladder usually owns it. Just a few years ago, most people in Dallas, Texas couldn't have explained what Lasik surgery was, let alone where to go to have the procedure. Now, thanks to Dr. William Booth, not only do those with perfectly good eyesight know what Lasik is (the word surgery is no longer needed) they also can name the most branded Lasik doctor in town. Dr. Booth successfully branded his practice in the formerly little-known category and soon, other Lasik providers quickly followed. The top three rungs in Dallas for Lasik are all reaping the rewards of Dr. Booth's pioneering firsts in branding his practice.

What's your specialty?

Step one is to determine your category/ladder, and confirm who, if anyone, currently occupies a position on that ladder. Remember: you're not just a dentist...you're a pediatric dentist, or a cosmetic dentist, or a sedation dentist. Be specific.

Next, evaluate whether the top rung on your specific ladder has been taken. Remember that who you most respect or who professional peers regard most highly is irrelevant. What matters is who's first in the minds of consumers.

One way to determine who, if anyone, is on your ladder, is to go to a local mall and ask the first 100 people you come across to name people or practices in your healthcare category. If you're shy, or just too busy, ask at the next Saturday morning soccer game or when you're out to dinner with friends. It won't take long for you to establish who has effectively captured mental real estate in your category. If you see an open ladder, jump in and become the market leader. Establishing leadership through your branding will give you a secure spot on the top rung that you get to keep unless you carelessly fail to take care of business and lose your brand-leader status through neglect or atrophy.

If you've discovered through this exercise that the top three rungs are occupied and you're stuck deep on the ladder, you can develop a sub-category and become *first* there. This is what I call a ladder within a ladder. A great example of this is Subway. They came on the scene when the fast food ladder was completely saturated. So, they developed a new sub-category (no pun intended) and became first on their new ladder of healthy fast food. Remember Dr. Cowgill, the "smile" dentist? That's just what he did. He established a new ladder within cosmetic dentistry and became the dentist who wants to see you smile! As we mentioned earlier, taking a spot on a mature ladder is tough business. It requires great focus and commitment. It can be done, but I recommend that you instead try to find a wedge or an unoccupied position where you can establish your business as the healthcare practice that people think of first when they need the services you offer.

MEGA CHANGES / MEGA CHOICES

We've already touched on the many changes that have occurred recently in healthcare and we know more are certain to follow. Changes are coming at such a furious pace that even the so-called experts can't accurately predict what to expect. Change happens everyday, even if we're not paying attention. If you have a pretty white picket fence and you ignore it, over time, you'll have a dirty rotting fence. There's no point in complaining:

change is unavoidable…
what matters is your response

You can choose to adapt and make change work for you, or you can be chained to the past, do nothing and fade into obscurity.

My chiropractor, Dr. Randy Butler has had his practice in the same office for 24 years. He recently learned his building would be sold and his lease would likely be terminated. This left him facing the unsavory challenge of either leasing in a different building nearby, or striking out once again as if he were starting all over. His location was in an increasingly aging and undesirable part of town, but it was also convenient for most of his patients. Knowing that he could be jeopardizing the number of patients on his books, he made the brave and daring choice to move to the newer, nicer end of town and renew his practice in a way that reflects a clinical but spa-like atmosphere. This was not what his older patients had been used to. It was a farther drive for them, but he decided to shoot where the ducks were flying and reinvent himself after all these years. "Change has been an ordeal," Dr. Butler says, "and was costly, but I feel I still have many years to go as long as I manage my practice properly. My move has made a statement to my patients that my practice is here to stay."

He has indeed lost a few patients who can't bring

themselves to drive three minutes farther down the same street or who think he's gone to the "high-fallutin" end of town. But most of his former patients have followed him because he's a great chiropractor and new patients are finding their way to him every week. He's moved out and moved up this late in his career because he embraced the changes that were forced on him.

One significant change that you just can't afford to ignore is the ever-increasing dependence on social networking. We have become a Facebook, Twitter, MySpace, YouTube kind of world, and by the time this book gets in your hands there will be new and even more targeted technologies. A growing number of consumer activities are being transacted online – everything from buying clothes, to researching cars, to selling homes. Increasingly, more restaurant orders are being placed online and via texting. Payless Shoe Source now texts targeted customers with special coupon offers. If you don't have the code texted to "insiders," you don't get the deal. Eventually, patients will be scheduling appointments through texting. If you're not tech friendly and are unwilling to "play" the social networking game, it's going to cost you. Many doctors and healthcare professionals have a Facebook page these days … and most of their Facebook pages say absolutely nothing. This is occupational suicide. By leaving what should be a constantly updated, moving and grooving site unattended, you're sending a message that your practice is DOA. Either maintain, update and sell yourself on that site, or get rid of it.

Dr. Thomas A. Brooks is an anesthesiologist in Springfield, Missouri. Even in Springfield, he realized that he had to set himself apart and adapt to changes all around him. One would think that an anesthesiologist could just sit back and wait for the business to come to him. Not so. Dr. Brooks realized, "No matter who you are, you have to market yourself if you want to grow your practice." He became a pain management specialist and opened a targeted pain clinic. He was one of the first to do this, and he did it exceptionally well. Because he was filling an obvious need, he caught the attention of a big hospital in town that realized they were losing business to him. He's now sitting comfortably because that big hospital bought him out. Win/win!

Change isn't your only battle ... there's also the enemy of choice. We live in an era of mega choices. The number of competitors has exploded exponentially in every category, whether you're a garage door company or a gastroenterologist. Consumers are being given more choices than they can shake a stick at even when it comes to something as specialized as sleep clinics.

Choice has become such a defining factor in the marketplace that it has created its own industry. There are countless publications, websites and surveyors who help us make our choices these days. Things like Consumer Reports, WebMD, Angie's List and Fodor's Travel Guides are all in place to help us make the best choices. A friend of mine moved to the U.S. from Romania. She tells the story of how she visited a grocery store to buy shampoo shortly after arriving here. She literally slumped in the aisle and began to cry when she saw the number of choices. It was too overwhelming for a young girl from a country where she had stood in line for hours just to get the last loaf of day old bread. And ... this was 20 years ago. Imagine how the shampoo aisle has grown since then.

I loved Cheerios as a kid. Every trip to the store, Mom would pick up a box of Cheerios. You know, the yellow box with the oat flavored cereal in it. Today, Cheerios has added Apple Cinnamon, Yogurt Burst, Honey Nut, MultiGrain, Frosted, Berry Burst, Fruity Cheerios, Cheerios Crunch, Chocolate Cheerios, and more! The same thing has happened to another American classic, Oreo cookies. Last I counted, Nabisco was making more than 30 options for us, not including the special holiday versions. Your children or grandchildren are growing up in a different marketing world than you or I did.

Consider all the choices that are increasingly coming into the marketplace for healthcare…

Patients can visit:

- the local ER
- a quick care/after hours facility
- their local WalMart or CVS to see a doctor at the 24 hour pharmacy
- the grocery store down the street for their seasonal flu shot
- a mobile Life Screening unit in their church parking lot

Or …

make an appointment at a private practice, with someone they know and trust

Up to a point, it's nice to have choices. But we are becoming so saturated in choices that confusion is inevitable. When it comes to healthcare, patients are practically paralyzed by the number of choices afforded them. It is causing such confusion, that many people are ignoring their opportunities for health maintenance and simply waiting until they have a problem that won't go away. The "doc-in-a-box" revolution that's moving to a location near you will only serve to confound them further. Wal-Mart, CVS, Walgreens and many others are currently adding on-site doctors to their locations. They have taken another bite of the patient services apple and are working hard to be "all things to all people." Now your patients can pick up motor oil, a can of Pringles and get that nagging cough treated by a doctor while they sip their favorite frappucino. Are you going to respond like Chicken Little and scream "the sky is falling," or are you going to be energized by the fact that these drive-thru doctors can't hold a candle to the personalized care you can provide?

GOLD IN THE HILLS

You have an exciting opportunity. It's California Gold Rush time! Back in the Wild West, there were those who pioneered and those who settled. There were only three major hits of gold. The first to the scene were the ones who struck it rich. Are you willing to be a pioneer, or will you be just a settler who waits until it's safe? Pioneering is risky business. They were the guys with all the arrows in their back. But, they were also the ones who got all the "good stuff." They were there **first!**

Thankfully, there are significantly more than three hits of gold in healthcare, and there are plenty of open ladders. You don't have to literally be first to own that mental real estate we talked about. You just have to be the best at claiming and communicating "first."

Leadership can be an important component in any marketing campaign because consumers believe if you're a leader, you must be better. So, like Dr. Cowgill, you may be the 50th dentist in your zip code, but the first to deliver a great smile. You may be the 10th walk-in quick care practice in town, but the first with on-site labs, specialized physicians or personalized follow-up care.

The attribute of leadership has been useful with BrandsFormation® client PTP (Physical Therapy Partners.) They have established leadership in pediatric therapies for their entire region. They did so by being first to communicate their "benefits focused" message to the community. They have effectively stated that they're number one, without ever using those words. Here's some of PTP's actual ad copy to give you an idea of how this works:

"I'm Brian from Pediatric Therapy Partners and together with over 20 other therapists in Speech, Occupational, and Physical Therapy, we're proud that more moms and dads trust us to help their children than any other practice in North Dakota. Your child deserves the best and most comprehensive help available. Trust your "mom instincts." Pediatric Therapy Partners – always reaching further to help your child laugh, love and live life to the fullest."

Here's the thing: you have the competitive advantage over whatever changes and choices flood your market when you occupy a top rung of your ladder. You can do this even if you are brand new in the market. Let me rephrase...you don't have a choice but to do this if you are brand new in the market. And like my chiropractor friend, you can adapt and create a new ladder ... old dogs can be taught new tricks. It's up to you. Remember that your prospective patients are searching for you in an often overwhelming sea of choices. How will you stand out? How will they find you?

The same tenacity that got you through all the years of preparation to arrive where you are today will be crucial to help you develop your brand. You've built a good local practice. Now don't stop until you've transformed it into a great local brand.

BRANDSFOR℞MATION
Branding Prescription:

- Being FIRST is not necessarily about getting to the marketplace FIRST with your product or service, but about getting into the minds of consumers FIRST.
- Each category, whether a product or service, has a mental ladder that consumers subconsciously rank top brands on.
- A Mature Ladder is one where most consumers can readily name a business or product in a category (i.e. banks)
- An Open Ladder is one where people are hard pressed to name a business or product in a certain category (i.e. podiatrists)
- Determine your category. Be specific. If you find your category is open, jump in and become the healthcare practice that people think of FIRST when they need the service you offer.

www.brandsformation.com

3

The Elevator Speech

("Going Up")

The 1988 movie "Working Girl" stars Melanie Griffith, Harrison Ford and Sigourney Weaver. Griffith's character, Tess, is an entry-level secretary who has aspirations of advancing her career. Tess seizes a moment to make a play for her client's big guns with a marketing idea she has developed. She has the amount of time it takes for the elevator to reach the ground floor to make her case to the executive in charge. She speaks quickly, directly and from the heart … and guess what? The CEO is convinced that he has found someone who can offer his company something special … something different … something better. Against all odds, Tess gets the corner office. Now that shows the power of a great **elevator speech (E-speech.)**

How long does the typical elevator ride take? Well, unless you're heading to the top of the Empire State Building, the entire ride should be less than a minute. Thus the term elevator speech. You don't have to literally be in an elevator to deliver one. It can happen anywhere. Start thinking of the world as your elevator … and be ready.

Whether you realize it or not, you're already giving **E-speeches**. Truly anytime you are given a moment or two to make a first impression, you use an **E-speech**. It may be personal or professional, and most likely it's not very good. Most people don't have a great E-speech simply because they haven't thought about it and they certainly haven't taken the time to carefully craft one.

The truth is, EVERYONE needs one. And what's more, as a healthcare professional, you need an E-speech more than ever. The future of healthcare is anyone's guess. No one can tell us for certain what to expect or what the full impact will be of the deep and drastic changes that are coming – changes that are literally out of your control. So where do you focus your efforts? **You go straight to the thing you can control – your brand.** You especially need to develop a razor sharp message to set your practice apart in the minds of everyone you meet. By answering the questions: Who are you? And why should I trust my healthcare needs to you? … you are giving your E-speech. If you do it well, you win!

The Harvard School of Business teaches this practice to its students and it is a key part of what I teach my BrandsFormation® clients. In fact, the Harvard School of Business says everyone needs an E-speech, whether it's for funding, grant writing, getting a loan or for entrepreneurs pitching their ideas to investors. An E-speech launches the process of awareness among your prospects. It piques their interest and leaves them wanting to learn more about you and your particular brand of service. Think of it as a "conversation starter" – something to lead to further interaction or more discussion. The whole point is to have a clear and intriguing message you can share to set your practice apart in the minds of everyone you come in contact with. If you aren't solving a healthcare concern, making someone's life better or filling a need of some type, you're wasting everyone's time.

So, Where Do You Start?

<u>**Consider Others:**</u> Begin by considering your audience. Who are you attempting to attract? What types of cases are you wanting to treat? Then, consider your competition. Who do you have to "outgun" in your market and what words or phrases do they own? What are they NOT saying? It's time to broaden your thinking. Be careful not to just think of the other healthcare professionals who share your title or degree specialization. Keep in mind that your patients and prospects will be subconsciously comparing you to every kind of healthcare professional they've ever visited, and in many cases any type of service they've ever received. Typically, those operating in any type of healthcare facility or practice tend to link their success to the outcomes they provide medically. Patients, however, are measuring largely on their perception of their overall experience. So concentrate on the "what's in it for me" advantages as seen by your patients.

In the book *If Disney Ran Your Hospital*, the call to redefine your competition is urged. "As long as we define our competition only in terms of our product, namely superior clinical outcomes, we will see our competition as other hospitals that are doing no better or worse than we are ... define your competition for customer loyalty as ***anyone the customer compares you to.*** And for every patient or family that has been to a Disney property and had a magical experience, Disney has slipped into their minds and become your competition."

Make it Compelling: A good E-speech will drive prospective patients toward a course of action. Please understand that there is a huge difference between ***benefits*** and ***features*** here. Features tell me what you do, what credentials or technological capabilities you have ... whereas benefits tell me how those things will make my life better, easier, healthier, more comfortable. For example, who would you rather go to for cancer treatment? A facility that says, "We treat all types of cancers and we have been around for 40 years," ... OR ... a clinic that says, "We have been fighting complex and advanced cancer for decades with Care That Never Quits®" (Cancer Treatment Centers of America.) This is a great example of why **words matter.**

See the difference? If your E-speech is not benefits focused, it is absolutely dead on arrival and your prospective patient has just moved on to find a more compelling story.

Your prospects collect thousands of "feature based" messages a day ... give them what they're hungry for ... a benefits buffet. List what sets you apart from your competition. Ask yourself what main contributions you can make and what problems you can solve. Ask friends, family and maybe even a few loyal patients to help you identify what makes you unique.

FEATURES = "so what?"
BENEFITS = "tell me more!"

Hear this! If you have degrees from the best schools in the country, or you have the latest technology, or you've performed more Lasik than anyone else on this planet, it doesn't matter if you cannot convey to me what all of that means in terms of how *I'm* benefited. I'm not trying to ruffle feathers here, *I'm trying to get people to care about what you can do for them.*

Two examples of this appear on the websites of very prominent healthcare facilities.

… mission is to serve all people through exemplary healthcare, education, research and community service.

Remarkable People,
Remarkable Medicine.

I'm sure they each paid a pretty penny for someone to craft these meaningful phrases that go a long way to build up their institutions. However, where patient benefits are concerned, they completely miss the mark.

I have never heard someone say they chose a particular healthcare facility because they have "remarkable medicine." Make me care … what will education or community service or remarkable people do for me?

Remember, every time you have an opportunity to make a first impression – whether it is in person, on your website or social networking sites – you are giving your version of an "E-speech." If you are not telling me how you can fill a need or make my life better – don't waste your time or money.

It's not as easy as it sounds. For grins, start paying attention to websites, social networking sites and advertising to see who you think hits the mark and who misses all together.

<u>The Right Hook:</u> It's time to take all of your benefits and net them down to the most compelling ones. With an elevator speech, you only have a few seconds to hook your audience and keep them interested. Most people will only walk away with 2-3 sound bites from a conversation. Does your E-speech convey what the unique benefits are of your practice in 60 seconds or less? Does it make prospective patients want to know more? If your E-speech has too many benefits, the latter benefits will begin to replace the primary ones and you will have lost your hook.

When you reach this point, economy of words is paramount. They must be few and they must be impactful. What words do you want to own in the minds of your prospects? Again, always be benefits focused. ***Make your E-speech an integrity based message*** … don't say anything that isn't true, or that is even slightly exaggerated.

Keep it Simple: To do this, you need to be able to net down the unique aspects of your practice in a way that will entice prospects to learn more about you. It's a hook, not your whole story. Write it down. Use concrete language and avoid terminology that your listener won't recognize or understand. However, don't be afraid to paint a vivid picture with your words. Beware of the pitfall of trying to be too clever. You don't want style over substance to silence your message and leave your prospective patient unengaged. Communicate the benefits you've identified. Using your compelling words, make sure that you stand out, you seduce or entertain. Will your prospect remember you? Be energetic, but not cheesy. Let your E-speech show passion for your profession, but don't come off sounding like a high-pressure salesman.

What's in a NAME?

Even the name of your practice can present itself as an E-speech. Your name should tell people who you are and what you do. Often a name can be an instant turn-off. One example of this: Dedman Hospital (I'm not making this up.) It took awhile but someone finally figured out that people probably don't care to check into a hospital with the word "dead" in the name. What about War Memorial Hospital? Now there are two words you don't want to see or hear when checking into a hospital…war and memorial!

If your last name is Cryer or Payne or Bloodworth, you should strongly consider reserving your ancestral pride for a coat of arms at home, but not your shingle. Here are two winning examples:

Stress Relief Psychology
Smiles For Life Dentistry

These both tell me what they do and how my life can be made better!

Deliver the Goods: Practice your E-speech. Is it too long? If so, take out a few words and go back to the drawing board. Get comfortable with your E-speech but don't memorize it lest it come off as a canned speech.

Keep it Fresh: As healthcare changes and technology increases, give your E-speech a fresh coat of paint. Come back to it and test it to make sure it's still relevant, it's still true, still compelling. Remember, with websites, on-line reviews and social networking sites, you'll now be giving your E-speech 24/7.

A WELL-CHECK for your E-Speech

Once your E-speech is ready, give it the **OPEN** test:

O: OMG IMPACT – Is it compelling? Does it tell me who you are and why I should trust you with my healthcare needs? Does it urge me to find out more about you?

P: PASSION – Does it reveal your passion for what you do? Is it memorable?

E: EASY – Is it easy to say and simple to understand? Is it easy for the listener to identify the benefit to them?

N: NEED – Does it fill a need or solve a problem for me?

Start thinking of how you can take this message and tie it into everything you do in your practice. This can include everything from how your phones are answered, to your signage, your website, your e-mail signature and even what your social networking profile says about you. I will guide you through this in subsequent chapters.

Once your E-speech has passed its physical, begin to practice it over and over until you can comfortably deliver it in any situation out in that worldwide elevator!

BRANDSFOR℞MATION
Branding Prescription:

- *Consider the world your elevator! Through your website and social networking sites you are giving a version of an E-speech everywhere you turn.*

- *A great E-speech is benefit (patient) focused as opposed to feature focused.*

Give your E-speech the OPEN Test:

- ***O: OMG Impact.*** *Is it compelling? Does it tell me who you are and why I should do business with you?*

- ***P: Passion.*** *Does it reveal your passion for what you do and is it memorable?*

- ***E: Easy.*** *Is it easy to say and easy to understand?*

- ***N: Need.*** *Does it fill a need or solve a problem?*

It's a 24/7 world...what are you saying to prospective patients?

---

www.brandsformation.com

4

Measuring Success

(Your 25% Bonus)

BrandsFormation® is your safeguard against the mistake many businesses make: the tendency to believe – falsely – that it is better to do something...anything, than to do nothing! In reality, it may indeed be better to do nothing rather than to do the wrong thing. Boarded up steakhouses and "out-of-business" signs posted in storefronts are a sad testimony to what often happens when business owners fail to brand and fail to marshall their resources wisely.

There's often a tendency with small business owners to think small and therefore stay small. They will buy a half-page ad in the high school yearbook, sponsor the 3rd grade girls soccer team, put up one billboard, advertise on radio the week before a big sale and limp along wondering why they aren't growing.

That's the way many business owners approach their marketing plan. They know something needs to be done but they just don't know what. The bad news is, most of the methods people apply to a marketing plan don't work. The good news is I've been doing this for more than 30 years and I've spent millions of dollars branding businesses in numerous categories. I have experienced many successes and a few failures. I call these successful failures, which means I've learned from my mistakes and I know what works. I can't tell you how to safely extract a tooth, align a back or transplant a kidney, but with certainty I can tell you what will work for branding your practice.

When you are held accountable for results and you're in the trenches, you find out what works and what doesn't or you die. The proven strategies are few and they are simple. So why isn't everybody using them? Typically, it's because they are committing one or more of the three biggest blunders in marketing:

1. Not measuring ROI
2. Media Mix-Up
3. Microwave Mentality

How many businesses claim to be best? That's nothing new. It's also not something most businesses can back up with a benefits focused message to the customer. Many claim it, so it's not a memorable message and rarely can "best" be validated or proven. One of my hard and fast rules is: *Don't claim something you can't back up.*

The same common mistakes keep being made by different people in different industries in different markets…but the failures are the same. It costs the same amount of money to deliver a "so what" message as it does to say something that will make prospective patients pay close attention and remember you.

There are three major blunders that I see made by most business owners in marketing and sadly, private practice doctors and healthcare professionals are no exception. Again, it's because you were taught everything you needed to know in school about diagnostics and procedures, but you were taught *nothing* about growing and running a business. Amazingly, if you'll just avoid making these three common mistakes, I can make your current advertising budget work 25% harder for you. (And that doesn't even take into account what kind of momentum you gain when you start doing the *right* things.)

ADVERTISING BLUNDER #1
Spending advertising dollars without knowing how you will measure the return on investment (ROI)

There's a scene in "Alice in Wonderland" where Alice comes to a fork in the road. She meets up with the caterpillar sitting on a mushroom. Naively, Alice asks the caterpillar which road she should take. The caterpillar questions, "Where do you want to go?" Alice replies, "I don't know." "Then any road will do," answers the caterpillar.

Are you an Alice? Do you fall into the same trap that many business owners do of throwing your hard earned dollars at seemingly "good" advertising options but having no idea where you're headed? Trust me, you're not alone.

I see it all the time. Business owners budget for and spend literally hundreds of thousands of dollars that they earned through sacrifice and sweat...and sometimes tears, on advertising their business. Yet, when I ask them the following questions ...

- *How much do you spend on advertising each year?*

And

- *Are you getting a good return on investment (ROI) with your ad dollars?*

It is a very rare occasion that anyone has an acceptable answer to the second question. Not only do they not know how to measure ROI, they're not really sure what ROI is in the first place. If you don't know whether something is working and you've been slinging money at it for awhile, you might as well take a long weekend and head to Las Vegas. Frankly, your chances of recouping your money are better in Vegas than in the crap shoot that is your current marketing plan. I'm here to tell you that you don't have to throw your hard-earned dollars down a black hole. You can confidently map out your advertising and marketing plan without fear of taking the wrong fork in the road. All that's required is to...

BEGIN WITH THE END IN MIND

You have to know where you're going in order to get there on time and in one piece. BrandsFormation® is the map to get you there. It also shows the way NOT to go. I have a golden rule when it comes to advertising. I strongly urge you to adopt it for your practice:

Never spend a red cent on any advertising until you first know how you are going to measure the ROI.

So what are you going to measure? That will depend largely on your goal. Why are you advertising in the first place? Do you want:

- more patients?
- better cases?
- growth of your practice?

- loyalty from current patients – based on patient retention?
- more referrals?

The key is to start off with some type of measurable goal in mind and know what the end is supposed to look like before you ever set off on your journey. Focus on what you want your advertising to return to you and quit acting like advertising money is just another necessary evil like your malpractice insurance. Your ad dollars can and will work for you with BrandsFormation® leading the way.

Allergy Associates of Wisconsin was enjoying an acceptable amount of success due to their regional referral network bringing in patients from neighboring states and even Canada, yet people in their own backyard didn't know they existed. Their goal was to expand beyond the reliance on referrals and start to let the average Joes with allergies know they could have an end to their suffering. Allergy Associates had a goal, embarked on a BrandsFormation® campaign and experienced a 50% increase of new patients coming from within a 20 mile radius. This happened in the first year. That's great success and measurable ROI.

ADVERTISING DOESN'T HAVE TO BE A GAMBLE

It is common for marketing plans to be determined over a great "free" lunch from an advertising rep that's been squeezed in between patients and drug reps who all want "just a little piece" of your precious time. Whoever gets to you last, or at your weakest moment, gets the nod and your entire marketing plan has been based on the "last tag" theory. This is a reactive approach and will very rarely reap any reward or ROI.

So, determine to be proactive! BrandsFormation® is a system that helps you leverage your limited advertising dollars and results in mindshare – owning mental real estate. No matter who your competitors are, you can be the practice people think of first when they need your service.

Where do you begin? It's the same principle as finding your way to a particular store in a big mall. You could wander aimlessly around the entire mall hoping to eventually bump into it, or you could go to the nearest mall directory and look at the map. Once you locate the store, you're off and running right? Wrong. First, you have to find the little green arrow that says "YOU ARE HERE." You can't get where you're going without first knowing where you are.

The same is true with your strategic advertising plans. Before you can decide where you want to go, you have to figure out exactly where you are today. This might be a bit painful, but the road to wellness often is. Take some inventory and honestly assess your *present reality.*

AD BUDGET TEST:

1) Determine how much money you've spent in the past year trying to reach people in your area. This includes television, radio, *Yellow Pages,* magnets, team sponsorships – everything.

2) Multiply it by 3 (for years) — this gives you roughly 1,000 days that you have been telling consumers that you exist. Now, if you ask 100 people, "Who comes to mind" when you mention your key words

or phrases, will it be you…or your competitor they think of?

This is your three year *present reality*. It will be your point of reference and comparison as you move through BrandsFormation®. After seeing that number, can you say that your dollars have been put to good use? Have you had a good ROI? Most likely, your *present reality* is leaving you a little disheartened right now, or you wouldn't have picked up this book in the first place. Let it go, we're on a fast track to improvement and measurable success, and we've got more mistakes to uncover. This is a bit like pulling off a Band-Aid, I know, but press on.

ADVERTISING BLUNDER #2
Media Mix-Up

The term Media Mix has proven to be one of the most "mixed-up" strategies around. At the surface, it makes sense. We all can appreciate the "don't put all your eggs into one basket" warning. By spreading around our advertising dollars, we have more opportunities to get our message across, right? Not so! What we have are more opportunities to throw our money away. Don't get me wrong; I am all for expanding marketing opportunities and getting your message to the masses through various mediums. However, in an attempt to diversify their advertising opportunities, many small business owners contract Little Bit Syndrome … do a "little bit" of TV, a "little bit" of newspaper, a "little bit" of direct mail, a "little bit" of radio. Consequently, nothing has had a fair shot at dominating or punching through.

View your advertising budget as a pitcher full of water. Each of your advertising efforts will be poured out into various media "cups." Every advertising vehicle represents a cup, so you have radio cups, e-mail cups, newspaper cups, TV cups, etc. Realize that even in a medium sized market there could be two or three newspaper cups, 20+ radio cups, and (thanks to cable) over 200 TV cups. Even if your pitcher is pretty large, how are you going to fill all those cups? The answer is, you can't. Better yet, you don't have to fill them all to be successful. This becomes a Baptist vs. Catholic issue. You can either baptize by sprinkling or baptize by immersion. Immersion is what we're after here. (You don't have to convert to a new religion, you just have to believe me. This works!)

In order to have a real impact and get the coveted prize of owning mental real estate, you must fill a cup; drizzling just won't cut it. The tendency is to invest in lots of different media vehicles (cups) and spread yourself around. But remember, success in branding is ownership. Own one cup before you move on to the next cup. Then, you will "pour into" that cup until you own it, and on it goes. You are free to *own* as many cups as you like; that represents the true sense of "media mix."

Why do you have to own each cup? It's simple. Every patient you're trying to reach is being bombarded everyday with an average of 5,000 messages. That means that 4,999 other brands are also splashing away, pouring their pitchers into the minds of your future patients. Do you really feel that special? Consider that many of those messages are being presented by such well known brands as Crest, Tide, AT&T and Ford among many others. And they're spraying them down with fire hoses compared to your little pitcher. Still feeling impressed with your advertising budget? Or are you feeling a little diluted?

YOU KNOW WHAT ASSUMING CAN LEAD TO!

The assumption by most people buying advertising is that they have to reach 100% of their market. Even if you were to capture mindshare in a market of 100,000 what would you do with that? It would be impossible for you to treat that many patients. But what would it mean to your practice if you captured mental real estate in 10% of the population? That would result in a minimum of 10,000 people who would think of you first whenever they needed the type of service or treatment you provide.

Meanwhile, the patients you have already attracted to your practice are being reminded why you are their best choice. So not only are you making your name known to those who've never heard of you, you are also helping build loyalty among those who already think of you first.

Another misconception is that it's best to use every available vehicle of advertising. Too many businesses are leaving tiny drops in too many cups! You'll never hear me recommend that. In fact, I would tell you to do the exact opposite.

What if you focused on one cup, put all of your marketing budget into it and worked it consistently over a long period of time? What if you pounded away consistently and frequently, dominating and cascading until you owned mental real estate and captured mindshare with that one cup? The result would be that the "drinkers" of that cup would know your message and have an emotional connection to your practice. They would *think of you first!*

Subsequent chapters will guide you in selecting the right "cups" and owning whatever "cups" you invest in.

Do you want to spend your advertising dollars adding to the white noise of thousands of discarded messages and hoping to make an impression on someone who happens to be listening at the exact same moment that they feel the needle sharp pain of a sprained foot and need the name of a good orthopedist? Or ... would you rather have a message that rings loud and clear with prospects who will think of you first whenever that foot pain interrupts their busy lives?

ADVERTISING BLUNDER #3
Microwave Mentality

I love baked potatoes. As a kid, my mom would bake me a potato for dinner and it would take about an hour. That seemed reasonable to me at the time. That is until the most popular Christmas gift of the '80's invaded every home and PRESTO ... a baked potato in 6 minutes. Wow, was I impressed. Now, like everyone else, I stand in front of that microwave pacing back and forth and complaining that the potato is taking too darn long. As the old saying goes:

Lord, grant me patience ... but give it to me NOW!

Isn't this consistent with the prevailing mindset of our culture? ***Instant gratification*** is what we all want these days. Industries and specialties have been born from this demand. That's why liposuction is so popular. Shortsighted and risk-taking people would much rather have their fat vacuumed out in a few minutes than to commit to a regimen of healthy eating and exercise to make a visible difference in their bulging bodies.

This same mentality has invaded every area of our lives and has successfully derailed many a marketing plan. Consider which of the following perspectives best describes your marketing mentality:

- ***Marketing Microscope*** ~ Short-term view of the "now." Simply concerned with filling the waiting room seats this month.

- ***Marketing Telescope*** ~ "Big picture" view of the marketplace over an extended period of time; planning well into the future.

These are two very different ways of marketing a private healthcare practice. Microscope practices will just be concerned with the here and now. I predict many of these will not survive all of the unidentified but imminent changes in healthcare. Telescope practices will stay the course, ***look into the future***, however uncertain that may seem, and stay confident as they wait for their coming rewards. Branding is measured in years, not months and certainly not weeks!

As a healthcare professional, you've probably waxed eloquent with many patients about things that are not good for their health. Alcohol, sugar and lack of exercise can all feel good in the "now"....but the consequences can stack up pretty rapidly as these habits are frequented and accelerated. Things that are good for you, like healthy eating and exercise, tend to work the opposite way. We see no immediate result. Can I do a four-mile power walk and drop 20 pounds in a day? Can I skip lunch all this week and suddenly slim down to my college weight? You get the point. Good things come to those that wait.

My grandfather, Melvin C. Morsch, was a very successful farmer in Hinckley, Illinois. I remember watching him plant corn, DeKalbXL45 to be specific. Do you think he ever came back the next day or week after planting and complained, "This isn't working"? My grandfather had common sense. He knew there was a time lag between sowing and reaping. The same holds true for branding. It takes patience, but the harvest is a blessed event.

Time is the friend of branding, and one of the essential elements of working a strategy. State Farm Insurance didn't brand "Like a good neighbor" into people's minds with a 13-week advertising campaign. They've been saying it for more than 30 years. They've been reaping the rewards of branding for many of those 30 years, but more importantly, they've been committed to their long-term strategy and consequently, they've staked claim on the mental real estate in consumers' minds.

If you've been operating with a Microscope Mentality, it's time to trade it in for the Telescope Mentality. With a laser focus on long-term commitment, you are ready to dive in and truly begin to brand your practice.

Thus far we've uncovered why it's important for your practice to be branded, the advantages to being first, the necessity of an E-speech and how to measure success while avoiding common mistakes. Now you're ready for the "how to" phase of the process. The BrandsFormation® system is comprised of four fundamentals, each of which is crucial to becoming the healthcare practice people think of first.

They are:

1) Strategy
2) Strategy Based Message
3) Consistency
4) Dominant Frequency

In the following chapters, I will give you a working knowledge of each of these fundamentals and will guide you through specific ways to implement them in your own practice.

BRANDSFOR℞MATION
Branding Prescription:

Avoid the three biggest blunders:

#1: Spending advertising dollars without knowing how you will measure the return on investment (ROI.)

My Golden Rule: Never spend a red cent on any advertising until you first know how you are going to measure the ROI.

#2: Media Mix-Up. Don't fall into the trap of doing a little bit here and a little bit there. Focus the budget you have on one medium and "dominate" that medium.

#3: Microwave Mentality: This is the desire for instant results. Branding takes place over the long haul, not in weeks or months, but in years.

- Adopt a "Telescope" mentality in marketing: Big picture view of the marketplace over an extended period of time; planning well into the future.

---

www.brandsformation.com

5

Strategy

(It Drives Everything)

Strategy is about survival …

In my all-time favorite Broadway musical *The Music Man,* Professor Harold Hill stirs up the whole town with his energetic and convincing "Oh, we've got trouble… right here in River City. That starts with T and that rhymes with P and that stands for POOL." Everyone remembers this song about trouble with a capital "T," but few people remember what he said prior to singing that famous song. "Well, either you're closing your eyes to a situation you do not wish to acknowledge, or you're not aware of the caliber of disaster indicated." He was referring to a pool table in their community that he warned would be the moral decay of their youth, and his answer was to start a school band. (Of course, to avoid "disaster" River City needed to purchase band instruments which – surprise! – Professor Harold Hill was marketing.)

Well you've got trouble, but I'm not peddling band instruments. As a matter of fact, I have nothing else to sell you…you already bought the book! The *trouble* you face is the turbulent and uncertain future of healthcare.

I can't write or produce a Broadway musical, but BrandsFormation® can and will help choreograph a vibrant, growing practice that will make your current and future patients stand up and applaud. You don't need catchy lyrics, but you do need one key thing: a **strategy**. In a turbulent, highly competitive healthcare world, strategy can be the difference between survival and d.o.a. for your practice. As we've discussed, it's not how good you are at what you do, it is how good you are as a marketer.

The first fundamental in your branding process is strategy, and truthfully, everything hinges on this. If you blow it on strategy, everything that follows will be out of sync. Strategy is that "something" that identifies your practice as individualized, special and different. It is a long-term plan of action that is designed to help you succeed. Strategy is about choice and how you proceed will affect the outcome of your practice not only today, but three, five, ten years from now.

Strategy is about perceptions…

Obviously you are strong in analytical skills. That's a great thing when it comes to science and procedure, but not as useful when it comes to marketing. Analyticals are all about the facts. Facts are important and without them we'd all be swimming in a sea of chaos. However, it is imperative that you understand that facts, in most cases, have nothing to do with what causes a patient to come to a particular practice and what causes them to stay loyal to that practice. It has to do with perception. Why? Because we are emotional beings and we act on those emotions.

Emotions are the horse and the facts (or logic) are the cart. Both are needed, but emotion is out front. Logic helps us to justify our decisions.

As we've already discussed, very few people walk in asking questions about your credentials. If they care that much, they've already done their homework. At the first point of contact, they are assimilating perceptions about your practice, about you, your staff, your wall color, the sights, sounds and smells of your physical space and the "feel" they get by being there. So, where strategy is concerned, I'm going to ask you to not get bogged down by the facts. Let me explain.

The average patient at the average hospital, in most cases, does not have the technical knowledge to judge if the doctor who just operated on their kidney is a genius when it comes to kidneys or has the steadiest hand in the O.R. So, they end up judging the ***procedure*** – and spreading word of mouth about their ***experience*** – based on how they "feel" the hospital food tasted or whether they "feel" they liked the wallpaper in their semi-private room. All of your schooling, training and background point to the focus on procedure, yet you're being judged on the perception of the overall experience. Talk about unfair. From the moment a patient pulls into your parking lot, to the first point of contact with your staff, their wait time and even whether they like the magazines you have available for them to read, you are being judged by the emotional responses that follow each interaction. Some of these variables are completely out of your control and many happen apart from your knowledge, input or physical presence.

Dr. Lawrence Cairns, who provided the Foreword

for this book, runs a thriving gynecological practice in Southwest Michigan called *FemmeVitale*. He has practiced medicine for decades. He has all the qualifications, the updated technology and the expertise to position himself as a doctor any woman should be happy to have treating her most complex and private healthcare needs. But, Dr. Cairns didn't rest on that. He realized that the patient perception, "how patients really feel," would be paramount to his success.

He knows that women need a caring professional to listen to their concerns, care about their comfort and overcome the challenges of their changing bodies. Cairns says, "You see, my profession has undergone immense changes from what it was just a few short years ago. Technologically, we're way ahead, but not all of the changes have been positive. To me, it seems as if a lot of the caring has gone out of the profession. But I made a vow to myself that I wasn't going to let that happen to my practice. I became a doctor because I cared and I don't want to lose that." Caring translates to trust in the eyes of a patient.

Dr. Cairns has expressed his strategy of "caring" to his patients through a welcoming and relaxing office décor, indirect and soft lighting, warmed examining tables and private dressing rooms. Can you imagine a woman going in to her gynecologist for the dreaded annual exam only to leave feeling she's actually been pampered?

He has all the latest and greatest technology; he has the years of experience and the most up-to-date training. All of these things matter a great deal. They should be the foundation for any healthcare professional. Although Dr. Cairns highlights these features to his patients on his website and in all of his marketing, his take-away message is about how much he "cares." *Caring* is his strategy. The great thing is that it's not just a strategy, he really is who he says he is ... he backs up his promise.

And that's why strategy is all about perceptions. What patients think about your practice – or should think about it – becomes word of mouth advertising. You need to do everything in your power to control the words people use when they are talking about you, since they are now "walking, talking billboards" for your practice. Do you like what those billboards are saying?

Take the time to actually observe what a patient experiences when they walk into your practice. Are they greeted properly and warmly? Are they given clear instructions? Do they find a clean waiting room and treatment area? Will they receive follow-up after tests or a procedure? All of these are called TouchPoints and will be discussed in detail later. Seeing the world through your patients eyes is one of the most powerful things you can do to help you develop your strategy and consequently brand your practice.

The 3 Steps to Building a Great Stratgey

1) Consider Your Competition:

Great strategy dictates that you never start with you. Great strategy starts with the competition: who is out there, who is known for doing what they do, who else is on the mental ladder in your category?

Strategy is finding the most advantageous position

Understanding who your competition is and what they are saying about themselves will help you build your strategy. Whatever benefits they are claiming, you want to claim something different. If you go in looking and sounding like someone else, chances are all of your marketing efforts, and more importantly your marketing dollars, will only help reinforce their message and drive patients to think of *them* first. OUCH!

The truth is that you may be better than your competition. You may have higher quality staff, greater facilities, better credentials and you may believe that all of these "truths" will win the battle against your competition. They will not! These have nothing to do with strategy. Again, we're talking about perceptions (which are held as truths in people's minds) and you need to have that patient perspective when you evaluate your competition. Your competitors may be doing a terrific job and they may have just what many patients are looking for, but I promise you there are weak spots. Identify just one of those weak spots and you could have the beginnings of tackling the next step to building a great strategy:

2) Finding your Difference Maker (DM)

Is there an idea you can own? Can you be a specialist pioneering something that will build your reputation? Why should people come to you instead of your competition? In the 2008 presidential election, Barack Obama – a first-term U.S. Senator from Illinois with only two years on the job – campaigned on only one word: Change. This won him the Presidency, and you don't need to be reminded of the overwhelming impact he's already having on healthcare in America.

From presidents to pizza the strategy method is the same. Pizza is a highly competitive and mature ladder in the marketing world. Pizza Hut was the family-oriented business, Domino's owned the words "Delivery in 30 minutes or less" and Little Caesar's was the cheap, two-for-one pizza that college kids loved because they had money left over for beer.

Papa Johns asked the question, "What's our difference maker? How can we stand out? Wait a minute: this is food and nobody is talking about the taste, so our strategy will be the best tasting pizza." Their slogan? "Better Ingredients ... Better Pizza ... Papa Johns." They have been the fastest-growing franchise in America for seven years.

A great healthcare example is my good friend Dr. John Gomez in suburban Dallas, Texas. He saw an opportunity to create a strategy aimed at patients (and even ER doctors tired of crazy hours) and created the first walk-in clinic in his area with RapidMed. He has provided an urgent care facility right in the middle of a booming residential area which at the time of his opening had a few standalone physician offices and a poorly perceived hospital about ten minutes away. By being different, FIRST, he is still enjoying a growing practice and in spite of other urgent care facilities opening up just down the street. Now those other urgent care facilities have to consider him and what they can do to be different from RapidMed. There's room for others on this ladder, but they have to use the kind of strategy Papa John's used and just figure out a new wedge and what they have to offer that is *different.*

RapidMed has offered such a successful alternative that it has become, in many ways, the new family practice model. As the other urgent care facilities were popping up all over town, Dr. Gomez and his staff realized that they had to be wowing patients and cementing their loyalty to RapidMed making it an uphill battle for the new guys to pry away the patients Dr. Gomez had already won over. Current and future competitors now have to make sure they can differentiate themselves from RapidMed or all their efforts will benefit RapidMed.

There's also my long time friend and branding pioneer Dr. Gustav Lo who saw the need in his town for laser hair removal services so he decided on a strategy to be the first laser hair removal center to spend money and brand. He has been highly successful, not only for being first but for following a strategy focused on the needs of patients. Now, Dr. Lo still gets to take care of patients and enjoy a good living without the additional responsibilities of fighting for a spot on the ladder!

Look at your business from your current patient and potential patients' perspective. You know you're unique, but trying to define how you're unique can be difficult.

Consider the following for brainstorming your Difference Maker:

- Think of three words to describe your practice.
- What are your values? Virtues?
- What's your story…how is it different from others?
- What are some of your beliefs, sayings, philosophies?
- Do you have any unique achievements? … first, best, newest?

Keep working at it until you are describing you and only you … if your DM sounds like any of your competitors, go back to the drawing board.

3) Get the word out

The third and final step in building a strategy is to get the word out: let people know who you are and what you do. The goal is to communicate to the public your "brand" and why patients should go to you vs. all the other people out there who do what you do. Strategy is the first fundamental in the BrandsFormation® system to build your good local practice into a great local brand. The next three chapters will walk you through how to get the word out … step by step.

Every successful practice starts with doing these first two steps: determining a business **strategy** and clarifying the **difference maker** that will make you stand out in people's minds.

Maybe you're a dentist tired of just drilling and filling and you decide on a strategy of becoming a cosmetic dentistry specialist with a needs-based clientele vs. walk-ins or emergencies.

Remember, once you decide on your difference maker, we have to put that into a word or set of words that quickly, clearly and powerfully describes you and communicates what you are all about. The process of taking your strategy and turning it into a message that is memorable, salient and impactful is what we discuss in our next chapter on creating a **strategy based message**.

WORDS MATTER

Let me repeat…words matter.

They compel people to make a buying decision. Remember Barak Obama's one word campaign … ***CHANGE.*** Not only do the words matter, they can flat out alter the outcome of your business. If you are going to live by the sword, you might just die by the sword, unless you deliver on your promise.

BRANDSFOR℞MATION
Branding Prescription:

- Strategy is about perceptions. Perceptions have more to do with why a patient comes to a particular practice and what makes them loyal than do other factors.

- Great Strategy is easy to understand and easy to communicate.

Building great Strategy:

- Begin by understanding your competition. Identify their weak spots or a void you can fill.

- Keep in mind that you want to look at things from the patient's point of view.

- Find your Difference Maker (DM.) Is there an idea you can own? Again, why should people come to you over your competition?

If your DM can be claimed by any of your competition, keep searching – it is not a true DM.

---

www.brandsformation.com

6

Strategy Based Message

("Look Ma, No Cavities!")

Once you've determined your **strategy**, the next step is to craft that strategy into a memorable word or set of words that tell your story to everyone. This is where you develop and apply your **strategy based message (SBM.)** Your SBM helps you "get the word out" about who you are and why I should choose you as my healthcare provider. Think about your **Difference Maker** and how you can communicate that succinctly and cleverly to your prospective patients.

A real homerun with a **strategy based message** is to own a word or phrase in marketing like Volvo = Safety or BMW = The Ultimate Driving Machine. They both represent a concrete understanding of what the consumer wants from the product AND they both back up their claims. When it comes to a word or set of words, you can have something image oriented like Nike's "Just Do It," but only if you have Nike money to put behind it. "Just Do It" doesn't tell me what Nike does or why I need to buy from them... but they've got the colossal ad budget to overwhelm consumers with visuals of athletic icons like Tiger Woods and make their **SBM** more about the image they portray. Their words are memorable, but only because of the money they've put behind them. Because you don't have the same Nike budget, you must make sure your **SBM** tells your story dead on!

Now in the chapter on **E-speeches**, you learned how to make a short and impactful presentation of who you are and what you do with a focus on benefits, not features. Sound familiar? Maybe you've already done your homework and have written an E-speech; if not, no problem. I've had clients whose E-speech has been the catalyst for their **strategy based message**, but typically, the overall strategy is determined and the E-speech is born from that. It can, and does work either way.

"What's the difference in an E-speech and an SBM?", you wonder. Well, mostly, it comes down to number of words and the vehicle of delivery. In every other way, they should be compatible. The take-away message should be the same, and that message should absolutely characterize and dramatize your **difference maker**.

You look to your **DM** or **strategy** to craft your **strategy based message**. Are you more convenient, more available, more focused on health maintenance vs. disease management ... what makes you different, better than your competition?

The ultimate **SBM** can come through your business name alone. For instance, *Smiles for Life Dentistry* says it all. Dr. Cairns, who I mentioned in the previous chapter, has done just that with the name of his practice. He had been a successful OB/GYN for decades and had delivered hundreds of babies. Having also attended to many women who were struggling with their ever-changing bodies, he realized that he wanted to focus on their needs and address their very specific health concerns practice wide.

His **strategy based message** is essentially the name of his practice: *Femme Vitale.* His E-speech expands on his SBM. It says: "Empowering women to jump over the hurdles of life breathlessly."

Thinking back on our mental ladders, imagine what a tough time Crest toothpaste had in the 1950's when they came on the scene against Colgate which had occupied the top rung for almost three quarters of a century. At the time, Colgate was using the word "cleaner" for their **SBM**: *cleaner breath, cleaner taste, cleaner teeth.* Some marketing genius for Crest realized that the idea of cavity protection was wide open, thus the strategy for Crest was born. If you're over 40, surely you remember the TV ad with the excited kid running into the arms of his mother in the dentist's office exclaiming, "Look, Ma, no cavities!"

That was followed by a man in a white lab coat reciting the statement proudly displayed on every box and every tube of Crest toothpaste. The American Dental Association's verdict was, "Crest has been shown to be an effective decay-preventative dentifrice that can be of significant value when used as directed in a conscientiously applied program of oral hygiene and regular professional care."

That's a strong **difference maker**. Another important point is that any fluoride toothpaste could have claimed the same statement from the ADA, but Crest did! Today, there are over 35 toothpaste brands on the market. Many of them tout their preventative abilities, but it's way too late to own that set of words because Crest was the first to claim "cavity protection" in the battle for consumers' minds.

Another important lesson from this particular example is that Crest stuck to their DM and made sure their

strategy based message was simple and clear. They didn't worry about communicating other benefits and features, they stayed focused. For instance, Crest would have never made it to the ladder with a toothpaste kids couldn't tolerate the taste of. So they made sure their toothpaste tasted appealing. That's a great feature, but it wasn't their Difference Maker and they didn't drive that feature home in their messages. They made "cavity protection" their SBM and they stuck to their guns.

Keep in mind that your SBM has to be laser focused. Your other important features will shine through in your practice, but you can't say everything that's good about what you do in your SBM. You must stay focused and choose words that are easily remembered and create an emotional connection. The more you focus, the more you'll have to give up highlighting other features and benefits. This doesn't mean you can't offer or perform other features or benefits, it just means they need to be the happy surprises your patients encounter when they visit your practice or your website. Remember, the big payoff comes through owning a word or set of words. There's just not room enough to tell your whole story in your strategy based message.

There are two criteria your **strategy based message** must meet:

1) Is it something only you can claim?
2) Does your **SBM** give the prospect a reason to buy?

Criteria #1

What you say must be different…
Are you the only one who can claim this message?

Having a great set of words isn't necessarily a golden ticket. If you've spent hours carefully crafting your words only to realize that you're saying what your competition has already been promoting, you've wasted precious time. So, again, I urge you: don't start with you! Always start with your competition. Know up front what your competitors are saying so you can say something different. If you think it's okay to sound similar to someone else, consider this:

Many years ago, there was a well-researched advertising case study that focused on Goodyear and Goodrich tire companies. They both advertised during the Super Bowl. At the time, studies showed that Goodyear was a clear number one brand in people's minds and Goodrich a distant second at best. Since the names were very similar, both started with "good" and both even had two syllables, guess who received the credit for both brands' commercials? You got it, Goodyear. They were the "original" and had gotten into the minds of consumers first. Looking or sounding at all like your competition will most likely cause your hard-earned marketing dollars to benefit them, not you.

Criteria #2
Give people a reason to buy!

Linda Thayer, the advertising giant behind hugely successful ad campaigns like Toys R Us *"Where a kid can be a kid"* and Clairol *Herbal Essence* with the famous shower scene, has said that you have to deliver a "BIG BANG" to your message. This is absolutely great advice, but people can make this their only objective and then fail miserably. With your **strategy based message**, you want to own a word or phrase that's both clever and compelling. Give your prospects a reason to choose you over your competition.

Clever without the compelling part will only lead to a brief second of listener entertainment and no emotional connection to your brand. How many times have you laughed out loud watching a truly entertaining commercial on TV, only to realize at the end, you had no idea what they were selling or worse yet the name of the advertiser? The best litmus test of a successful ad is not whether it was creative, but whether it increased your sales. If it doesn't resonate back to your bottom line, regardless of how many people comment on it, you have a bad **strategy based message** on your hands.

The use of humor can be powerful OR it can be downright useless. There is only one reason to use humor ... to dramatize your **difference maker.** If you use humor just for the sake of getting attention, you will bomb out. I live in Texas, and if you've ever visited Texas and been outside for any amount of time, you've most likely become acquainted with one of the most dreadful creatures on earth: the fire ant. Every Texas resident with a yard hates fire ants. That's why the following Ortho radio ad was a colossal success.

Fire Ants are not lovable. People do not want Fire Ant plush toys. They aren't cuddly, they don't do little tricks. They just bite you and leave red, stinging welts that make you want to cry. That's why they have to die right now. You don't want them to have a long lingering illness...you want death. A quick, excruciating, "see you in Hell" kind of death. You don't want to lug a bag of chemicals and a garden hose around the yard...it takes too long. And "baits" can take up to a week. No, my friend, what you want is AntStop Orthene Fire Ant Killer from Ortho. You put two teaspoons of AntStop around the mound, and you're done. You don't even water it in. The scout ants bring it into the mound, and here's the really good part: everybody dies! Even the queen! It's that fast. And that's good. Because killing Fire Ants shouldn't be a full time job, even if it is pretty fun. AntStop Orthene Fire Ant Killer from Ortho. Kick Fire Ant butt!

That's superb use of humor because it's funny but, more importantly it dramatizes their DM. Sure, I'm entertained by this, but mostly, I'm compelled to run out and buy a bag of AntStop Orthene Fire Ant Killer from Ortho to get rid of the wretched insects that covered my feet in painful, itchy sores.

Benefits vs. Features

You can clearly define and communicate a DM that can translate into a memorable **strategy based message**, and still miss the mark by a country mile. This is where the benefits instead of features warning comes into play. Your DM must actually make a difference in the lives of your patients and prospects or you've completely struck out. Thankfully, this can be easily avoided. All you have to do is focus on patient needs and then fill a hole.

What are some of the challenges patients face?

- CONFUSION: Who can help me with a particular healthcare need? What do all the changes in healthcare mean to me? How do I begin to find the right doctor for my needs?

- SCHEDULING: Who can see me before or after work hours? I can't hire a babysitter for my kids just to go to the doctor. What if I can't make an appointment during a weekday?

- TIME: I'm too busy to think about scheduling an appointment unless I'm really sick. What if I make the appointment and the doctor is running late? I can't afford to be away that long.

- LOCATION: This can be a big challenge for some and not the least concerning to others. Many patients will gladly go the extra mile (or 20) if they really like, trust or respect their healthcare provider.

- RESPECT: It works both ways. They need to respect you, your expertise and recommendations, but they also need respect from you. Patients don't want to feel condescended to, rushed or dismissed.

Recently we were having dinner with my cousin and her husband. He is in the insurance business and deals with many healthcare providers so he understands how tight time can be in any given practice. It surprised me then to hear him say, "If a doctor ever makes me wait more than 30 minutes, I'm never going back. My time is valuable too."

Imagine the damage that is done to your "branding" and your name when a patient is accidentally scheduled on a holiday, or your receptionist logs a different time on the schedule than she did on the appointment card and the patient is told they've come at the wrong time. Not only is the patient most likely finished with your practice, they also have a story to tell about you, and the word of mouth they spread, fair or not, is completely out of your control. As obvious as these things may seem, I have recently heard these complaints. Studies have shown that customers will share a positive experience with an average of 2-3 people, but they will tell 11 or more about a negative experience.

Everyone is starved for time and a universal top five complaint with any healthcare practice is the "wait time." From this patient need, you might position yourself as the "No Wait" doctor. I understand that this may force your staff to be creative with scheduling and diligent throughout every business day, but if you can deliver on the promise of not wasting your patients' time you'll be getting so many calls you'll need to turn some of them away. That's a good problem to have. While you're at it, you may want to implement a ban on the use of the words "waiting room." There's no reason to remind people that their time is ticking away.

Focusing on patient needs helps you to hone your **strategy based message** into something that stands out in that sea of 5,000+ messages they hear daily. You can have all the bells and whistles of a great ad campaign, glossy print and cutesy jingles and not come close to capturing mindshare.

The most compelling deterrent to patients choosing you could be as plain as the nose on your face. Think about their needs and their perspective, not yours.

ICONIC VS. ECHOIC MEMORY

It's important to understand how memory gets stored to assure that your SBM is working for you in capturing mindshare. Sight and sound memory are your two greatest channels into the minds of your prospects. Neurologists call these:

Iconic Memory: Sight based ("icon")
Echoic Memory: Sound based ("echo")

Iconic memory refers to what comes into the mind through sight. Our sense of sight is so vivid and important to us that it's easy to assume it is the most important source for our memories. Not so. Echoic memory is the result of what we hear. Contrary to what most people would think, what we hear is retained in our memories much longer and more accurately than what we see. Why? Because it takes up to five seconds to store sound, while sight is stored in one to two seconds. Since sound takes longer, it is far more accurately stored and more easily recalled.

Both of these can work for you to get into the minds of prospective patients, however, echoic memory is proven to have more impact. It has been stored with more accuracy so the memory lasts longer. Consider a study that was conducted several years ago on behalf of car insurance companies. The purpose of the study was to gauge how eyewitness accounts of car accidents compared to one another. When interviewed, out of 10 eyewitnesses only 1.7 people would agree on what they *saw*. However, when asked what they had *heard*, the average number that agreed shot up to 6.7. This told the investigators that sound was delivering a more accurate account. This should tell you that what you say and the words you use matter a great deal.

Helen Keller was blind and deaf since before her second birthday, and basically cut off from the outside world until she met Annie Sullivan. Annie found a way to break through the silence and open up Helen's world to communication through sign language. If anyone can truly compare the relative value of sight and sound, it would be Helen Keller. This is what she said:

"The problems of deafness are deeper and more complex, if not more important, than those of blindness. Deafness is a much worse misfortune, for it means the loss of the most vital stimulus – the sound of the voice that brings language, sets thoughts astir, and keeps us in the intellectual company of man."

Haven't you had the maddening experience of not being able to get a jingle or a song out of your head? The memory is triggered by cues. That's why an entire song can be brought to mind by merely giving someone the first line, a couple of bars of music, or even an unrelated but similar few words. That's why most of us learned our ABC's through a song.

That's the power of intrusive sound which we call echoic memory. That's also why the United States Government in 1970 outlawed cigarette ads involving sound. Cigarette companies found themselves at a severe disadvantage in their branding efforts as a result. Cigarette ads in magazines just don't carry the same punch as the rugged Marlboro Man backed by the theme from *The Magnificent Seven.* I'll even bet that from memories of old-time radio, your parents and grandparents can still tell you what "LSMFT" means. Ask them. "Lucky Strike Means Fine Tobacco," the radio announcers said ad nauseam.

These are some of the reasons I'm such an advocate of advertising with intrusive media: like TV and radio. To quote Jack Trout again, "People spend 85% of their time immersed in ear (broadcast) media and only 15% with eye (print) media." So shoot where the ducks are flying!

Next priority is to make sure that your message is compelling...that the message itself moves prospective patients to remember you, think of you first and ultimately call you for an appointment.

LOGICAL vs. EMOTIONAL

Some marketing professionals say that emotion is the primary buying motivator in almost every area. Others will say consumers buy based on logic. The professionals don't agree, yet the March 2009 issue of *Advertising Age* cited research that showed emotional campaigns are almost twice as likely to generate larger profit gains than logical ones. They also documented that emotional campaigns are effective at reducing sensitivity to price and that consumers get an increased sense of differentiation causing them to endure a brand and remain loyal more readily.

Inject emotion into your **strategy based message**. It has the ability to dominate rational thinking. Buying decisions are driven by emotion, then followed by justification through logic. Again, this can be compared to the difference between benefits (emotion) vs. features (logic.) Both are important, but one sells better than the other, hands down. "Look, Ma, no cavities!" provided both, which makes Crest's SBM such a great example.

There is a great debate about whether emotion or logic are more effective in branding healthcare practices. Truthfully, either can work. Take the example of two successful insurance companies: State Farm and Geico.

State Farm went for the emotional message of "Like a Good Neighbor, State Farm is There." Geico, however gave their prospective customers a logical reason to buy them, "Give Us 15 Minutes and We'll Save You 15%." Both companies own some serious mental real estate.

The more successful branding campaigns for healthcare professionals are going to master the art of representing both sides. In healthcare emotional connections are made through: humor, hope, compassion, relief, respect and dispelling fears ... logical connections are made with reference to: research, technical advancement, medical outcomes, convenience, and comparisons to others or testimonials. The following radio ad copy for Physical Therapy Partners exemplifies the merging of both connections:

Your child deserves the best *(emotional)* ***and most comprehensive*** *(logical)* ***help available. All in the comfort*** *(emotional)* ***and convenience*** *(logical)* ***of your own home! Most children learn, grow, laugh and live best*** *(emotional)* ***in their own natural environment; that's why we at PTP, make house calls!*** *(logical)* ***Trust your "mom instincts"*** *(emotional)* ***... call to set up your free screening.*** *(logical)* ***Pediatric Therapy Partners. Reaching further to help your child laugh, love and live life to the fullest!*** *(emotional)* ***SFX (Child Giggle)*** *(definitely emotional!)*

I've said it before, but I can't stress this enough...
WORDS MATTER

When creating your **strategy based message**, choose your words carefully. They are everything! What a single word conveys can be the key to a brilliant

BrandsFormation®. Don't use words that are dated, irrelevant, bland or cliché. The minds of your prospects will immediately reject your message. The goal is to connect and to capture mindshare. Use words that surprise, delight, shock, inform and get remembered. What works for nationally recognized brands can be applied here.

Nike = Just Do It
WalMart = Save Money. Live Better.
Subway = Eat Fresh
Sprint = The Now Network
Visa = Takes You Where You Want To Go
Volvo = Safety

In your local market, you can become just as recognized and just as "branded" as these instantly recognizable names. Dr. Terry Cowgill was the new kid on the block. He was up against many established dentists in his market. How would he be able to build up a brand new practice?

He decided that he would try something most dentists frowned upon: advertising. Dr. Cowgill knew that if he was going to put several hundred thousand dollars into a new dental practice and be successful, he would have to do something different. Because most people have negative associations with sitting in dental chairs, Dr. Cowgill's strategy was to be the dentist that patients associate with fun – not drills, shots, cavities, pain, fear and dread.

He wanted to be known as the dentist with a sense of humor, the dentist who makes you smile. He knew if he could make patients smile, his practice would grow. This was his DM. Now, he could have chosen to buy ads that said "Come see me, Dr. Terry Cowgill, because I'm funny and I'll make you smile." That would have been awkward and it would not have worked. Instead, with a little help, he realized he had to "say it, without saying it."

He began to sponsor a humorous radio show called *The Adventures of the Tooth Fairy*. That sponsorship ended more than 10 years ago and people still ask him today about the Tooth Fairy. Dr. Cowgill is now producing his own parody ads that are unique and have been extremely successful. He said, "People tell me they look forward to our new ads." Dr. Cowgill was able to make a connection with prospective patients by using humor to show he was a different kind of dentist. His **strategy based message**: The Dentist Who Makes You Smile! His practice has been a huge success.

Almost everyone has a website now. If you conduct searches online for practices in your area, you'll instantly see which, if any, of your competitors have gotten the memo on having a **strategy based message**. Most have no unified message, just a logo and tons of text. Some have way too many messages and appear to be trolling for anyone and everyone who might need them. Remember, trying to be all things to all people won't get you a rung on the ladder.

Below are some examples of messaging (SBM) from the websites of various healthcare providers. Presumably, these messages are there to tell people who they are and what they do. I have purposely left out their practice names because my aim is not to embarrass anyone, rather it is to show you how easily a set of words can make or break you.

Can you guess which of the following meet the 2 Criteria of a Strategy Based Message:

1) Is it something only you can claim?
2) Does it give the prospect a reason to buy?

Emergency Room. Without the Wait
Captures the benefit to patients

The Standard of Care Throughout the Continuum
What?

For the Smile of your Life
Bulls-eye.

Life changing care – world changing research
Words that have little impact on patients.

Five Star Treatment for your Heart. And You.
Solid focus on core expertise – hearts – but also on human beings.

We're dedicated to the exclusive care of children and teens with skin disorders
Anyone can claim this. Tell me why you're different.

Care That Never Quits®
Homerun … tells me they won't give up on me.

Expect a Miracle!
Remember one of my hard and fast rules: Don't claim something you can't back up.

Your **strategy based message** tells people who and what you are and why they should do business with you. This is how you get branded and you definitely want to be in control. If you don't do this effectively, you will be branded by others and by what they think of you. Take charge. Stand for something with your SBM or you'll fall flat on your face.

Your objective in taking this branding journey is to be the healthcare practice people think of *first* when they need the service you provide. With that in mind, use this template as a step-by-step guide to create your SBM.

F: FIND – Fnd and use words that only you can claim
I: INSPIRE – Does your message inspire patients to choose you?
R: REASON – Does your message give patients a reason to buy?
S: SOUND – Have you captured mindshare with the two major components of sound … music and voice.
T: TRIGGER – Have you chosen words that trigger memory and create your brand?

As you protect the consistency of your strategy based message, let me give you a simple word picture to keep you on track. I teach a process with each of my clients that I call **Bricks and Mortar**. Very simply put, it's a way to keep your SBM intact as you move through variations in your marketing plan.

BRICKS and MORTAR

Mortar represents the consistency of elements in your marketing message … the words you want to own in the minds of prospective patients, plus the consistency in your audio logo (both in voice and music) and print logo (both in color and in words.) This is the cement that holds your strategy based message in place. Mortar elements must remain consistent in every advertisement you deliver. These will include your strategy words, voice and music. Visually speaking, this can also include an emblem, color or symbol such as McDonald's golden arches. They have stayed golden for over 50 years because the arches are a mortar element for their brand.

Bricks are the stories that dramatize your difference maker and your strategy based message. They are always changing. Bricks give power to your message and better yet, they prove it. These bricks are your ticket to punching through and being memorable. People connect to stories and learn through them. Through the use of stories, you avoid the deadly hack clichés everyone talks about when asked "what makes you different?"

While your mortar elements stay the same, your bricks (stories) can, and should, change. My recommendation is to choose between six and eight bricks over a period of one year. Each brick should have a shelf life of six to eight weeks in your advertising before adding a new story, or brick. You will consistently beat the drum of your strategy based message, but the new brick will give power to that message in a new and equally compelling way. Together, bricks and mortar cement the connection between your message and mental real estate in the minds of your prospects.

Below are two radio ads from the same client. Notice the mortar elements (consistent) and the bricks (changing.)

AD #1: Do All You Can

MUSIC: UP AND UNDER ***(Mortar)***

*ANNCR: If your child had trouble eating, walking, talking – anything that kept him from developing his full potential, you'd do anything and everything to help him, wouldn't you? Unfortunately, many parents with children identified with special needs often think that taking advantage of our State's Early Intervention Program is doing everything they can to help. It's not. At Pediatric Therapy Partners, additional direct therapy resources are available and offer advanced help for your child. ***(Brick)***

*BRIAN: Many of our current patients at PTP have been surprised to discover how much more valuable help is available for their children beyond the State Early Intervention Program. ***(Brick)*** This is Brian from Pediatric Therapy Partners and together with over 20 other therapists in Speech, Occupational, and Physical therapy, we're proud that more Moms and Dads trust us to help their children than any other practice in North Dakota. ***(Mortar)***

*ANNCR: Your child deserves the best and most comprehensive help available. It's your child – your choice. ***(Brick)*** Trust your "Mom Instincts." Go to pediatrictherapypartners.com to schedule a free screening. Pediatric Therapy Partners – Always Reaching

Further – to help your child laugh, love, and live life to its fullest. ***(Mortar)***

SFX: (CHILD GIGGLE) ***(Mortar)***

AD #2: Your Child … Your Choice

MUSIC: UP AND UNDER ***(Mortar)***

*ANNCR: For most parents it's a moment they'll never forget. It's when your child is identified with having special needs. Your mind is flooded with questions and concerns. People make therapy recommendations. You go along because, well, you just don't know you have options when it comes to your child's therapy providers. But you *do* have a choice. Your child is not locked in to one of the big health systems in town. Or a specific insurance network – no matter what they may tell you. ***(Brick)***

*BRIAN: Many of our patients at Pediatric Therapy Partners have been surprised to discover they have a choice. ***(Brick)*** I'm Brian from Pediatric Therapy Partners and together with over 20 other therapists in Speech, Occupational, and Physical therapy, we're proud that more Moms and Dads trust us to help their children than any other practice in the North Dakota. ***(Mortar)***

*ANNCR: Your child deserves the best and most comprehensive help available. It's your child – your choice. **(Brick)** Trust your "Mom Instincts." Go to PediatricTherapyPartners.com to discover your options.

Pediatric Therapy Partners – Always Reaching Further – to help your child laugh, love, and live life to its fullest. ***(Mortar)***

SFX: (CHILD GIGGLE) ***(Mortar)***

****The voices are mortar elements. They stay the same. So does the music and the SFX of the child giggling. All of these echoic memory triggers help create a connection in the minds of prospective patients.***

With your message intact, you are ready for the third step in the BrandsFormation® process, **consistency**. This is where the rubber meets the road.

BRANDSFOR℞MATION
Branding Prescription:

Your objective is to be the healthcare practice people think of first when they need the service you provide. Use this template in creating your SBM:

F: FIND - *Did you find words that communicate your Difference Maker? Are they words only you can claim?*

I: Inspire - *Does your message reach people on an emotional level?*

R: Reason - *Does your message give patients a "reason to buy"?*

S: Sound - *Have you used the two major components of sound ... (music and voice) to enhance your brand and capture mental real estate?*

T: Trigger - *Have you chosen words that trigger memory and create a stronger brand?*

When you are ready to communicate your strategy based message, remember to keep your mortar elements consistent and use your bricks to dramatize and tell stories.

---

www.brandsformation.com

7

Consistency

(What the Golden Arches Can Teach You)

I travel the country trying to help people BrandsForm® their businesses. When I come rolling into Omaha, Nebraska and it's late, I'm tired and I just need to grab a quick bite to eat, I want something familiar and quick. I know I can always count on the "Golden Arches." A Big Mac and fries are going to taste the same no matter if I'm in Omaha or Los Angeles. I'm buying ***consistency*** … I know what's on the menu and what it will cost. I also know that those golden arches won't be hard to find. They're all the same. McDonald's is brilliantly consistent and their brand speaks for itself.

Businesses figured out a long time ago that in order to brand their products and gain customer loyalty, they had to be consistent. If you go to McDonald's in Hong Kong, guess what? The arches are yellow! They aren't painted red with dragons on them. McDonald's really set the standard for branding in the world of fast food and they practice it brilliantly everyday, worldwide!

I've talked to you about how easy the BrandsFormation® system is to implement. This is the fork in the road. This is where you batten down the hatches and commit for the long term. The first two parts of working the system, 1) **strategy** and 2) **strategy based message**, are fundamentals that require significant planning and thought. Part three, **consistency**, requires your vigilant attention and commitment to maintaining your brand and staying true to your message through all of your points of contact with patients and prospective patients.

NOT JUST A NAME OR LOGO

People get branding confused with logos and signage all the time. That would be the same as someone describing your personality and saying, "His name is Bob." That's not who you are. To truly achieve a brand, you must have consistency. You have to have the whole strand of DNA for it to amount to anything. Your name or logo do not a strand make.

Your brand is your practice's character or personality. To achieve consistency, you must make a concentrated effort to communicate messages to patients and prospects for the purpose of getting your brand to take up residence in their minds. This cannot be achieved through just your logo. Every corner of your office, every piece of direct mail, every greeting, phone contact, sign, webpage, radio/TV ad, every staff member must be helping to build a relationship between patients and your brand.

To be effective at this, everyone in your employ has to be educated about your DM, your E-speech, your strategy based message and what your brand is saying about your practice. Everyone on staff has to get it! Additionally, anyone who helps design, support or communicate your brand including your web designer, your print shop, your interior designer and any account executives that are selling advertising to you must participate. If they are not protecting your brand, you need to find someone who will.

When you practice consistency, you form an awareness of your brand with patients and prospects. This in turn makes them familiar with you which gets you considered. This is like the camel getting his nose into the tent – shortly the rest will follow. This is how you get considered first when they need you. Eventually, they've crossed over from prospect to patient and in their patient experience, that same consistency grows trust...they know what to expect. After you've delivered that consistent experience over time, you've achieved loyalty.

This directly affects your profit margins in two ways: 1) You aren't constantly having to replace and renew your patient list and 2) when you are consistent and patients know what to expect from visit to visit, you've effectively branded your practice and you can charge more. That's right ... leading marketing experts agree that a branded service or product can charge more because consumers are willing to pay more for what they know and trust.

WITHOUT CONSISTENCY, YOU HAVE CONFUSION

When you lack consistency, your prospects and patients get confused. They can easily start mixing your message with another message from your competitor and you've lost their mindshare. Your staff also gets confused about what the message is and then you've lost your support system. You get confused and you've lost your focus.

Consistency can be flubbed up all too easily. This is why it requires vigilance. If you are *Life of Smiles Dentistry*, you can't have a sour-faced hygienist working for you. If you're *Weigh Less Now Weight Loss Center*, your consistency is shot when patients are welcomed by a morbidly obese receptionist. I'm not trying to encourage discrimination of any kind, I'm just saying everyone has to buy in.

The loyalty patients have to healthcare providers has declined immensely in this present generation. Due to the overwhelming number of choices patients have, they become easily swayed and leave for something they think looks better. Then there's the colossal number of people who would love for a dentist, doctor or skin care specialist to call out to them with a positive, benefits based message so they could finally get help … they've just not known where to go.

The U.S. Department of Health and Human Services reports that more than 100 million Americans are currently living without any form of dental care. How crazy is that, when there are so many dentists who could be serving them? Perhaps nobody's told them "ignore your teeth and they'll go away." Given that preventative maintenance is so important in dental health, I'm guessing that many of them are just ignoring this item on their "to do" list and waiting to wake up with an excruciating toothache one day. Then what? How about you be the dentist that has been telling your story before the toothache hits? You might not only get a new patient who's desperate for help, you most likely will help many find you before the suffering begins.

CONSISTENCY = claim (helps you stake claim to mindshare)
CONSISTENCY = comfort (patients know what to expect)
CONSISTENCY = constancy (customer loyalty is established)

B.J. Bueno is my good friend and co-authored the book *The Power of Cult Branding*. This has led to the introduction of Cult Branding courses at Harvard Business School and MIT. He instructs how Cult Brands share a dedication to consistency through the following three variables:

LOOK – SAY – FEEL

The cult branding of such icons as Apple, Harley-Davidson, Oprah and Southwest Airlines seems unattainable on the local market level, but there are lessons to be learned from these powerhouses who boast of huge fan bases. Their customers want to do business only with them.

Bueno's research has uncovered the psychological foundations that lead to authentic customer loyalty. Over 90% of consumer behavior is unconscious. Even when asked directly, most people don't know why they do what they do. This can make market research and typical "branding" beliefs completely irrelevant when the wrong questions are being asked. You have to figure out what best motivates your patients, and then consistently deliver on those motivations through the above variables.

Let's take a look at Apple. Notice, I don't even have to add the word "computers" after their name. Everyone knows what I mean. They've taken what is easily the most popular fruit in our society and given us a reason to think instead about computers when we hear the word "apple." That's branding genius. In order to own that kind of mindshare, Apple has practiced consistency in their *look*, their *say* and their *feel*.

LOOK: Apple has taken a dull, black, industrial piece of technology and turned it into a sleek, hip and bright box of status!

SAY: Instead of using dry techie jargon that only means something to IT geeks, Apple came up with the simple but impactful slogan of "Think Different."

FEEL: Apple has created a feeling of belonging to something better. They have communicated a type of rebellion against the normal conventions of their industry which typically intimidates or alienates "outsiders." Apple embraces everyone. Their customers don't just become loyal, they become downright adamant that everyone should own an Apple.

HOW DOES THIS TRANSLATE TO HEALTHCARE PRACTICES?

Let's break down LOOK, SAY and FEEL as they relate to what you do to earn a living and uncover how you can be an Apple in healthcare!

See 360°
What people see when they encounter your brand

Remember "Iconic" memory? Take a look around … all the way around your practice. From your brochures, to billboards, to business cards to your physical site, your look speaks for you. Your See 360° should loudly proclaim your brand as you've defined it through your **strategy based message** and your **difference maker**. Your **See 360°**

encompasses all the visual aspects of your brand ... your curb appeal, your visual marketing like your signage, business cards, print media and TV ads. Figure out who you are and what you want to look like, then stick with it.

But don't stop there. This also includes the colors you use. People need to always see a consistent color or color combination (not close to it but dead on, same Pantone everytime.) They must always see a consistent logo. You should always use the same font and even the same sizing. No excuses. Don't hire some cookie cutter web designer who sells you what he's sold to three of your competitors and end up without your logo on your new website.

The use of consistent color and logo can dramatically impact how easily your brand is recognized and remembered. Consider how committed Coca-Cola has been to their logo and to the color red. In 1886, John Pemberton concocted the sweet syrup mixture that became the base for Coca-Cola. His bookkeeper, Frank Robinson came up with the name Coca-Cola and also wrote it out in the distinctive script that is recognized around the world today. They have stayed committed to their consistent look. Coke is arguably the most recognized brand in the world in part, because they are deadly consistent. People will only remember your name, your look, your colors and logo over a period of time. That's why you must keep driving them home.

Although there have been slight changes over the decades, the consistency in Coke's logo is obvious. It jumps off the page and exudes confidence. It screams "this is who we are, and you will love us" ... and we do.

Your curb appeal also matters. I once visited a new doctor who had come highly recommended. I almost cancelled the appointment when I saw that he officed in a strip shopping center with a "walk-ins welcome" sign blinking in the window. To me this spelled desperation. If he's all that great, why would he need to take on the gimmicks of a dry cleaner or liquor store? This particular doctor specializes in preventative and alternative medicine with the use of natural hormones for both men and women. People don't "pop in" for such visits. Most likely, he's padding his practice until he gets up and running with the types of cases he most wants to treat. Meanwhile, he's sending the wrong message to the patients he most wants to treat because he doesn't "look" like his specialization. Being consistent can be costly for a time, but it will pay off in spades down the road.

Walgreen's pharmacy chain is a great example of the See 360° of brand consistency. Walgreens are typically on a corner lot. You will find the same construction of the store, angled on the corner, with a neon lit pharmaceutical symbol behind glass over the door. Walgreens always uses the same large red letters and the layout of the store is always consistent.

Texas chiropractor, Dr. Randy Butler recently relocated and revamped his 25 year-old practice. His name stayed the same, but he realized that he needed to have a look and feel to his practice that was updated and set him apart from the many chiropractors he shared a zip code with. Dr. Butler has made use of a tree symbol to symbolize the "tree of life" and the strength and straightness of a healthy spine. Those words are not used, the message is simply implied. However, the look or See 360° part of his practice is consistent. The office has a serene and natural feel to it. Soft lighting and neutral colors are used. The tree logo is shown on his business card and simple tree paintings and touches of leafy greens are carefully placed throughout the treatment rooms. The staff uniforms are simple and neutral, no patterns to distract from the look of the office. The look is consistent, but not overbearing. Be careful not to get on a theme and beat it to death.

Say 360°
Your strategy based message and the sounds associated with your brand

This is the "Echoic" memory we discussed earlier, and it has a greater impact than the "Iconic" memory, although both are important. This variable in consistency is achieved through staying true to your strategy based message…your word or group of words that tell who you are and why I should choose you.

The words that appear on your correspondence, your business cards, direct mail pieces, billboards, radio/TV ads, and even in your greetings and farewells should consistently serve your brand! Have you ever been hesitating on something and someone tells you to "Just Do It"? I have, and every time I hear those words, I think Nike! They have so consistently branded those words that even when Nike isn't the topic and Nike isn't paying, if those words are used, they get the credit. Consider working your branding words into how your phones are answered, or how patients are greeted when they enter. Again, don't be overbearing. If you're branding yourself as "caring" the way Dr. Cairns has done, then you have to *sound* caring. When patients leave your practice, you should say, "Goodbye Mrs. Jones." Practices that sell "caring" know the names of their patients. If you're not going to deliver on your promise to be caring, then change your promise to something you can deliver on.

The Say 360° is identified through every written word, every spoken word and even the music that's played in your office. Consider too, that sounds you can't control can even be wrapped into the overall experience. If your other patients are bringing in screaming kids and talking on their cell phones or texting with the volume up, your atmosphere is affected. These are all matters that can and should be addressed by you and your staff to control the consistency of your practice as much as you can.

Touch 360°
The overall experience and emotional connection to your brand

This is the emotional part of the equation. Have you ever noticed how happy the staff in vet offices are to see your pet? Every time I take my dog in to the vet, the receptionist stops what she's doing to welcome her. The vet assistants and the vet himself are all so glad to see my dog. Wow! How nice would it be if the pediatrician was as happy to see my kids? I love my dog, but honestly, there's nothing that means more to me than for someone to make a fuss over one of my kids.

In the Touch 360° variable, you have every opportunity to stand out and make a positive impact on your brand. Most healthcare practices are sterile, serious and frankly, downright unfriendly. Think about it, nobody really relishes the thought of being a patient, and the nature of a visit to a doctor or dentist is often related to a stressful situation. Your practice could actually be a pleasant surprise to your patients.

We are living in a disconnected society emotionally speaking. What if you were the one face-to-face contact your patient had all day, and you were cold, harried, frazzled and aloof? That patient would not leave with a positive Touch 360° experience. However, if you spent a moment to warmly greet, smile and listen to your patient, you would be offering them a take away memory that positively impacts them, but additionally helps you even more in the mindshare you've helped to claim. If your patients consistently experience this kind of Touch 360° treatment, they become loyal to you and eventually, you've got a walking billboard for your practice that legitimately and accurately shares your message with others.

Touch 360° is riding on the attitudes and commitment of your entire staff. If they are not buying into the message that you want to convey, they can kill your chances of branding. Conversely, if you have only one or two staff members who go the extra mile and treat patients the way my vet treats my dog, they can **become** the brand. Yet, if you bank only on that one person carrying the practice, they just might carry the practice right out the door should they ever leave for a better deal down the street. In this case, turnover can truly damage you. Having consistent attitudes and standards of patient interaction can guard against this. It should not be a surprise to you that your front office can make or break you, and so can just one bad experience with a tech or nurse. Vigorously protect this aspect of your practice.

When your LOOK, your SAY and your FEEL all point to your strategy based message, you've achieved consistency in your message and are experiencing *media synergy* at its best. This is when all of your efforts come together and exponentially increase your exposure and recognition. Think of the mind as a wall and the message as a nail. What's going to go further into the wall? Hitting 10 different nails just one time, or hitting the same nail 10 times? The answer is obvious. This is how media synergy works.

10 consistent messages = Power x 10
10 different messages = 1/10th Power

CONSISTENCY ALSO MEANS STAYING THE COURSE

This is where many battles in branding are lost. People start out buying in to the concepts that I've shared and they strike out on a mission to BrandsForm their business. They put their time and energy into developing strategy, finding their DM and crafting a great SBM. They even go so far as to put together a really good advertising plan AND invest their hard-earned dollars to put the plan into action. A few months go by, several checks are written, and yet nothing much seems to have changed. Frustrated and disheartened, they throw their hands up in the air and walk away. Don't give up! So many bail out too soon and waste all the time and money they've spent. The payoff was around a few more corners if they would have just held on longer.

"A brand is not built overnight.
Success is measured in decades, not years."
~ Al Ries

In *consistency*, there are three stages to work through.

The first one is the hardest and takes the longest to complete. If I can urge you to trust me here, the patience that you exhibit in this stage will pay off.

RAMP UP: This can take one-two years. All of your energy is in this first effort. This is where the majority of business owners bail out and where the true battle is waged. Don't give in to a "microwave mentality." Think long-term.

RESPONSE: Here's where it gets really exciting. People start talking about you and start mentioning they've heard about your practice, they've seen or heard your ads and you are becoming the buzz about town. Mindshare is starting to be realized.

RESULTS: This speaks for itself! More new patients are coming in and patient retention is increasing. Suddenly you are bringing in better cases, and you're struggling less and less to make your practice work. Finally, you are free to experience the fullness of why you got into healthcare in the first place.

Many people stop short of carrying through. They come up with a great SBM and a slick way to get their message out, and then they stop. Failing to carry that SBM throughout your practice will kill your credibility. It's the same as not delivering on a promise. BrandsFormation® is not just about communicating who you are, it's about actually being who you say you are. You must avoid breaches of the brand. All aspects of your practice need to match your SBM. If you are Burger King and you say "Have it your way," then you must not get uppity with customers who place a special order.

Your staff can be one of your most valuable assets or your kiss of death, especially since you are not marketing a concrete product but a service (actually, you're marketing an experience!) Review sites prove this like WebMD and Angie's List. Most of what's talked about on these sites is how people are treated by other people ... the staff.

Assign and empower all staff to be on the lookout for inconsistencies or breaches of your brand. Giving them ownership will not only make them better employees, it will increase their motivation and it will streamline all of your staff to work together toward an understood and achievable goal. The relationship your patients have with the overall experience in your practice will become your brand, in their minds. That will have been delivered by you and each staff person in your practice. Therefore, it is paramount that every person who represents your practice is completely brand conscious ... and completely committed to protecting and even enhancing the brand.

When you consider how consistency is valued in all walks of life – in products, people, and experiences – the importance of implementing consistency in your marketing and delivery cannot be exaggerated. We value consistency as a character trait in people. In fact, most of us are downright intolerant of flighty and inconsistent people. Consistency is seen as a strength. The relationship you seek to build between your patients and your brand will be built on trust. That trust grows out of their consistent experiences with you and your staff delivering on the promises you've made in your consistent SBM. Don't waiver!

BRANDSFOR℞MATION
Branding Prescription:

You want to have a consistent LOOK, SAY and FEEL for your practice.

- ***LOOK:*** *From your brochures to your billboards to your curb appeal and four walls, consider your "look" at every turn to see what it says about you.*

- ***SAY:*** *Your Strategy Based Message (SBM) or the "set of words" that you choose must be consistent in all advertising, including your website and social networking sites.*

- ***FEEL:*** *The emotional part of the equation. The feel variable is riding heavily on the attitudes and commitment of your entire staff.*

When your LOOK, your SAY and your FEEL are all consistent, you achieve media synergy. Advertising dollars and efforts are exponentially more effective.

www.brandsformation.com

8

Dominant Frequency

(It's Not What You May Think)

One of the best salespeople in the history of the world lived over 2000 years ago. He only had a three year selling career, and then He was brutally killed. His name – Jesus Christ. Whether you believe in Him as I do or not, your daily life is impacted by His life and death. Your planner, your calendar and your birthday are all based on the date of His death. Today, there are hundreds of thousands of buildings we call churches that stand as a living testimony to the power of His message. He was selling a message. So how did He do this? Through parables or stories. People don't want to be sold, which is the method most salespeople use, but we'll all pause and listen to a good story. Our minds and hearts are open to stories and parables.

Facts "tell" – Stories "compel"

One of the criteria for your SBM, remember, is that it be true! Don't just tell a story for the sake of being compelling; you have to deliver on whatever you say or you're toast.

Once you have determined your strategy, crafted your strategy based message and are being consistent – both in what you are saying and how you are delivering on your message – you are ready to attack the final step in the BrandsFormation® system … **dominant frequency**.

You're looking for a group of people with whom you can communicate your message and share your stories in a long-term, consistent and frequent way. Having a powerful story can give your dominant frequency twice the impact. Powerful stories resonate with listeners and cause their ears to perk up.

I'm not talking about the kind of dominant frequency that heart surgeons look for in EKG's. This dominant frequency has to do with having a commanding presence in an advertising medium.

Total market dominance is obtained by the really big guns like Coca-Cola, Volvo, or State Farm because they have the deep pockets to buy every medium available. But you can achieve dominance on a radio station, or within a certain TV program, or by using the same print materials effectively and over an extended period of time. Keep in mind, where print is concerned, effective marketing is typically done here through specific products and timed sales like cars and mattresses. It doesn't hold the same effectiveness as electronic media for "planting the seed." Instead it falls more under the heading of "predicting the need."

After taking BrandsFormation® on the road for the past several years, I've enjoyed demonstrating how to brand in visual and entertaining ways. One visual I get frequent comments on is the Cup Parable – it's how I demonstrate dominant frequency.

For the demonstration, I use Styrofoam cups and a pitcher of water. Each cup represents one advertising vehicle and the pitcher of water represents the entire advertising budget of your healthcare practice. Visualize this as I explain. The cups are labeled according to how many different places you are spending money to get your "story" told. So, for example:

2 TV stations = 2 cups
3 radio stations = 3 cups
On-line search engine = 1 cup
1 *Yellow Pages* = 1 cup
2 billboard companies = 2 cups

You get the idea. Now imagine that all the money you've designated for advertising fits into that pitcher of water. Be honest with yourself about how big that pitcher would be and how much water that would really look like. As you picture this scenario, whether you have 2 cups or 10, imagine now sloshing a little bit of water into cup 1, then cup 2, and so on. How many cups are you trying to fill with your little pitcher of advertising dollars?

You are working with an advertising budget that's most likely limited to begin with and then you're watering it down significantly by dividing what's there into six, seven or even 10 cups. Is there any wonder that you don't see the results you want? Most healthcare practices are being advertised in this way, if they are advertising at all … and they are all throwing money down a dark hole. This is the "little bit syndrome" I spoke of earlier.

If you were going to build a swimming pool in your backyard, you would hire a professional pool builder – someone with a business card, references and a picture portfolio of the pools they had already built. You wouldn't slap down a $10,000 deposit not knowing that you were working with the right people. Well, imagine, after doing your homework and selecting a reputable pool builder, you look out the window to see a man with a little shovel digging a hole. If you're like me, your first reaction would probably be "well, what do I know about building a pool?" But if a few hours later you noticed that the guy had dug dozens of tiny holes with his little shovel all over your yard and left for the day, your concern would definitely escalate. It doesn't take a genius, or a pool builder, to figure out that's no way to dig a BIG hole. You could kiss your visions of a pleasant afternoon poolside goodbye ... and you could start your new improvement project, which would be how to cover up what looks like a serious gopher problem!

This is the same concept as my Cup Parable. You aren't going to achieve a decent ROI with little dribbles of advertising dollars in several different advertising cups. You've spent all your hard earned marketing dollars but nothing good has come of it. What a waste.

HOW MUCH DO YOU REALLY NEED?

First of all, you can't reach 100% of your local market ... and who says you need to? If there are 100,000 people in your market and you reach even 10% of them, that's 10,000 new people. Can you really handle that many new patients? How many new patients would it actually take for you to have a thriving, growing, healthy practice? What would it mean to your practice if you could completely capture the hearts and minds of even 5,000 new prospects and that many people thought of you first whenever they needed the kind of healthcare you offer?

I realize that you need to speak to far more people than you can logically handle on your patient list since everyone who absorbs your "story" won't necessarily act on it. But it's most important to identify who you need to tell it to. So that brings us to the question: Who says it's best to use every available vehicle (or cup) of advertising? Not every medium works well to begin with, then there's the issue of needing to target your audience.

Make sure that the medium you choose has the right target audience for your practice and beware of special "packages and promotions" that aren't consistent with reinforcing your brand. You and I both know that if we want a good deal on a mattress we can get one Memorial Day weekend, 4th of July weekend, or on Columbus Day of all things. I don't know about you, but I have other things (fun things) to do during holiday weekends and I may just decide in November that I need a new mattress. Don't get caught up in trying to predict when someone will "need" you. Remember ...

You're planting the seed, not predicting the moment of need!

Let's review the comparison between echoic and iconic memory. Iconic memory refers to the pictures that people retain whereas echoic memory is the sound that is retained. Echoic is the clear choice when it comes to recall, accuracy and the length of time the memory is stored. So start by putting your advertising dollars where the ROI is the greatest –intrusive media, or sound media. Quite simply, sound media (radio and TV) work the best for branding.

Now I know that you are being bombarded by a virtual parade of media reps vying for your business every week, but if you react to every offer, every proposal with value-added promos, free color printing, complimentary weekend spots, etc. ... you will be exhausting your ad budget before the ink dries on the contracts. This is where I unashamedly beg you to work only with people who have wrapped their brain around your strategy, your DM and your brand. If they are trying to change any of that, or in any way fall short of maintaining your consistency, do not work with them! Again, fiercely protect your brand and only work with those who will do the same.

Typical thinking is that business owners can't afford not to advertise in the *Yellow Pages*. First of all, can we really say "the" *Yellow Pages* anymore? There are so many big, fat, yellow books left on my front porch these days, that I don't know which ones to keep and which ones to line the gerbil cage with. For those three people in the universe who still bother to open a *Yellow Pages* these days, good luck finding what you're looking for. It's not user friendly. Take that money and tell your story to a world that's ***listening***!

The best *cups* for planting seeds are found in the electronic sound media like radio and TV. They are intrusive by nature ... you are not waiting for people to find you. Instead, you are going out everyday and finding them. These intrusive media can also be easier to dominate than print media because they are more cost effective and are targeted to specific audiences.

Nothing is forever and change is inevitable, however my experience is that dollar for dollar, effort for effort, radio is the very best way to deliver your message. TV works great too, it's just significantly more expensive.

Be aware that radio works differently than TV. Radio typically produces loyalty to a particular station whereas TV produces loyalty to particular programs on their station. Knowing this will help you to target your audience in terms of demographics, income and psychographic factors. This reduces the potential for waste and increases your potential for dollars to be focused on the right kinds of prospects.

Where radio is concerned you want to be sure and choose the right station. If you're a pediatrician, you want to find the station that more young mothers are listening to. Please do not choose your medium, be it radio, TV or print, based on *your* personal media consumption. Focus on who you want to target. Also, be aware that there can be a significant advantage to advertising on a "spoken word" format over a music format. This would include news and talk stations. The listening on these radio stations is more intentional and attuned than listening on music stations. However, this advantage is lost if your target audience can't be found listening to these formats – so choose accordingly.

So, what if you focused on just one cup – not one medium, but one cup within that medium? What if you pounded away, day after day, week after week, for months. You would be drenching the audience of that cup consistently with the message that explains to them why they should choose you! Eventually, you would own mental real estate in the minds of that audience.

Why do you think companies like State Farm and Geico keep pounding their same message year after year? They know that there are always new people to reach and that they must continue to reinforce the message with those who have already heard it. Why does McDonald's keep pouring it on via the same TV stations for us to watch over and over? Because they know it costs much more to start over again than to maintain what they've already accumulated in mental real estate. These companies are masters at being consistent and frequent.

So, with careful consideration, pick a cup and start filling it with your pitcher of water (your advertising dollars) and only pour into that one cup. It will take time and that cup must be overflowing before you even consider moving on. Extensive marketing studies have shown that the typical customer must have at least 17 impressions of a brand before they consider trying it. This is where dominant frequency comes in and works to your advantage.

You are going to get a group of people to start to recognize who you are, then actually hear your message and begin to make the emotional connection to your brand. Then you want to consistently remind them that you're there and that they need you. You will be having a conversation with them day after day, week after week, month after month.

In radio, dominant frequency is achieved when you get what's referred to as a ***3 Frequency***. This has been an industry wide standard for years, so all you need to know is that it's accurate and it works! A 3 Frequency means that the average listener will hear your message at least 3 times over a 7-day period. On the average radio station in America 25 commercials per week will yield a 3 Frequency. This allows for various habits of listeners. Again, it means if you buy 25 commercials on one radio station in one week, the average listener of that station will have heard your message three times.

Remember, studies show consumers need at least 17

impressions of a brand before they'll consider trying it. So, you're looking at a minimum of six weeks before the average person will consider you. You're most likely a "needs" based service provider, so remember that although listeners may recall you in six weeks, they may not need you for 6 months. Trust my advice and practice dominant frequency. It works!

Dominant Frequency also helps you measure success!

If you truly follow what I've laid out for you here, you will have an easy-to-evaluate marketing plan. Since all of your money goes into one cup, it will be easy to pinpoint whether that particular cup (medium) is working, providing you have given it a minimum of twelve months to be effective. When that one cup is full, you may add another cup. I strongly encourage you to add, not change. Changing will yield the same results that the pool builder with his little shovel would get. Once you have proven Cup #1, then added Cup #2, if there is not a bump in new patient growth, Cup #2 is failing you.

You have gone from shelling out gambling dollars, to naming a purpose for each of your marketing dollars. Now you are able to see how your money is working for you. Each cup can be measured individually and accurately.

Using dominant frequency, you will reap the rewards of following the BrandsFormation® system as I've laid out. To reiterate, you will have found a group of prospects to tell your story to and have a frequent conversation with. If you stick with it, eventually, you will own their hearts and minds and when they have a need that you can meet … BINGO … they think of you first!

BRANDSFOR℞MATION
Branding Prescription:

Focus your advertising in one "cup" for maximum success.

- Take the budget you have and "fill" or "own" a cup (medium) before you ever think about adding another.
- You don't need to attract 100% of the market. Think about what it would mean to your practice to reach up to 10% of the market.
- Don't get caught up trying to figure out when someone will "need" you. Remember ... you are planting the seed, not predicting the moment of need.
- Dominant Frequency will also be an aid in measuring success. Each cup can be measured individually and accurately.

---

www.brandsformation.com

9

Implementation

(You Can't Advertise Your Way Into Superior Performance)

REAL PATIENTS. REAL STORIES.

- Our doctor sent a letter to our family (and I'm assuming all of his patients) explaining that he was going through a very difficult divorce and a difficult financial period, but the rumors he was going out of business were untrue.

- We had been seeing my child's orthodontist for about 18 months when we showed up 15 minutes late for our regularly scheduled appointment. (We had never been late before, although we had patiently waited for him on occasion.) We were told by a very stern assistant that their "late policy" meant our child would not be seen that day and the next opening would be in six weeks.

- As a routine part of her doctor's visit, my mother-in-law was having her vitals checked. The pleasant nurse that was taking her blood pressure kept banging on the machine and complaining, "these things never work!"

- While visiting my doctor's office, I noticed a rat trap on the floor of the bathroom. Thankfully it was empty. For the rest of my visit, however, I kept expecting to see a rat scurry across the floor. I did not go back.

- We had to wait in a freezing cold examining room for almost 30 minutes. We commented on our discomfort to a nurse and she simply replied, "I know, it's the coldest room in the building." No apologies. No blanket. No nothing. She left and we continued to freeze.

- We walked into the office and the receptionist just continued what she was doing. She never looked up or even said hello. She just pointed to the paper and said, "Sign in."

- In the waiting area of my last doctor, there was a sign that read: If you have waited longer than 30 minutes, please tell the receptionist. That told me they had a plan in place to react to such a wait, but not necessarily a plan to prevent one. This may be acceptable to them as standard procedure, but I didn't accept it and I won't go back.

Each of these experiences will be retold over and over again. In fact, according to marketing studies, customers will share a negative experience with an average of 11 people. These situations are all avoidable. The solutions are common sense ... just not always common practice.

Your strategy based message will prompt people to ***think of you first whenever they need your service*** and it will likely get them to your front door. Once they step across the threshold of your practice though, they are yours to keep (or lose!)

You can put lipstick on a pig, but it's still a pig.

Brand loyalty is created through what you do, not what you say. Don't invite people into your practice through advertising until you are ready to ***"WOW"*** them so that you can keep them. Be your best internally, first!

You and your staff generate customer expectations through your brand promise. Being *unable* to meet those expectations, or worse, being *unwilling* to meet them can be more harmful than having no message at all. You simply must deliver on your promise.

You can't advertise your way into superior performance.

Rarely will patients complain to their healthcare provider about why they are dissatisfied. The majority will just leave and never return. Sometimes they don't even feel dissatisfied, and yet they leave the practice for something "better." There are three ***Levels of Satisfaction:***

Dissatisfied
Satisfied
More Than Satisfied ... a FAN!

Even satisfaction is not enough to retain your current patients; you need to go beyond the "satisfied" and create "fans" of your brand. As healthcare changes unfold and out-of-pocket expenses increase, your patients will be unconsciously increasing their expectations. Every aspect of what they experience in your practice will become a factor. Give them reasons to become "fans."

- ***Friendliness Factor:*** smile; give a warm greeting; kick it up a notch. I have noticed when I use the drive-thru at my local Chik-fil-A®, employees say "my pleasure" as opposed to "you're welcome." There's nothing wrong with "you're welcome" but "my pleasure" sounds friendlier and communicates they're truly grateful for my business.

- ***Go the extra mile:*** look for things that aren't necessarily in your job description; i.e. walking an elderly patient to the car…helping a frazzled mom by carrying the diaper bag or distracting a fussy baby.

- ***Do things others aren't:*** like Dr. Cairns and his warmed gel and tables.

- ***Follow-up:*** Text or call the day after. If support staff makes the call, mention the doctor's name. "Dr. Brown was wondering how you are feeling today."

- ***Create a powerful workforce of brand believers*:** everyone is required to produce ***"WOWs"*** for patients

This chapter will help you build a game plan and critical path timeline to implement what you've learned throughout this book. It is crucial for you to have a unified plan in your practice. Everyone in your employ must get on board and forget the autonomy they may have grown used to in what typically becomes an "I'll handle my job my way and you handle your job your way" type mindset. "WOWing" the customer is job #1.

Every interaction patients have with your practice affects their perception of your brand.

If their experience doesn't match what your advertising has promised, then you are committing breaches of your brand.

Every employee needs to understand what your brand is promising, but to truly partner with you, each of them must also *protect* that promise. If your Difference Maker is "We truly care about each of our patients" and the receptionist fails to make eye contact or share a warm greeting with patients as they enter, your receptionist is not protecting your brand. Every staff member must be vigilant in delivering the brand promise.

This will garner loyalty in patients, but also loyalty from your staff. It's a win/win. Not only will this allow for you to reduce turnover and costly training but, more importantly, it will foster a motivated staff that will aid you in the overall BrandsFormation® process.

Authorship creates Ownership

Tap the potential of your ***brand believing*** staff:

- Make sure they know and understand your brand's promise.
- Recruit staff members who possess the skills and talents to reinforce your brand.
- Make this part of your new employee training.
- Give them permission and encourage them to contribute ideas, and to perform great brand enhancing acts.
- Reward good brand building behavior.

You have successfully come through the acquisition of knowledge phase on BrandsFormation®. However, that won't improve your practice one bit unless you put it to use. Here's the game plan for implementation:

The Game Plan
AREAS OF IMPLEMENTATION

1) TouchPoints 360° Checklist
2) Strategy
3) Strategy Based Message

My pastor gave a great sermon titled, "Does Your Walkie-Walkie Match Your Talkie-Talkie?" He spoke about the disparity between what we say and what we actually do. We've been told since childhood not to make promises we can't keep. That rule works in life and in marketing: *your walk has to match your talk for success, in anything.* TouchPoints 360° Checklist is a tool to help ensure that your walk and your talk are aligned and "saying" the same thing to your patients. TouchPoints 360° is where I begin when I am working with a new client and the outcome is on my shoulders. If you will apply what I've taught you and follow these steps, you will see amazing results and your practice will grow.

TouchPoints

What's a TouchPoint? Harvard Business Review adopted the term "touchpoint" in 2007 to describe instances of direct contact between a customer and a service. Through branding, you create expectations. Your brand is your promise. TouchPoints are the vehicles that help you deliver on the promise. Each TouchPoint helps shape your patient's impression of you and therefore cannot be left to chance. This is why it's important you **start** here.

- Realize and communicate to your staff that every encounter a patient has with them leads to a TouchPoint – this includes phone contact, web contact, physical setting, advertising, etc.

- With every TouchPoint one of three things happen:
  1. A moment of ***MAGIC ("WOW")***
  2. A moment of ***MEDIOCRITY***
  3. A moment of ***MISERY***

- The TouchPoint 360° Checklist will help you guarantee moments of ***Magic***.

- After the checklist has been completed, begin with your weakest ratings first and start making improvements. This will serve as your working "to do" list.

- Don't just settle for all *Good* ratings … what can you do to move *Good* to *Great*?

Remember, patients are rarely coming to a healthcare practice of any kind under pleasant circumstances. They are typically coming to you because something is wrong. Whether they are injured or ill, under emotional or physical stress, or they're displeased with something, there are many places they would rather be than inside your practice. Make them glad they came to see you, even if their circumstances are tough.

To help you honestly assess your current performance, I have created the TouchPoints 360° Checklist. TouchPoints are the elements of a customer focused practice and a checklist is a diagnostic tool to help you determine areas of strength but also your trouble spots. This checklist/evaluation deserves more than a few moments of skimming the surface. Unless you are 100% healthy as a practice (unlikely) there's always room for improvement.

What's the first order of business when diagnosing a medical condition with a patient? Taking the vitals. I know this is not normally done by the doctor, but rather a function of the nurse or assistant. I'm going to ask you to take the vitals of your practice … I need you personally involved here. In fact, you need to assemble a Diagnostic Review Board. This must include you, your office manager or other key individual you trust to be in charge of implementation, plus at least one support staff member such as a nurse, technician or assistant, and two or three current patients (preferably one long-time patient and one or two new patients.) This Diagnostic Review Board will help you to honestly assess your areas of weakness and help you build on your strengths. The most important quality for them to bring to this process is honesty. They need to be able to deliver an honest critique on every measurable aspect of your practice, and you need to be able to truly hear and respond to that critique.

Evaluating each of the TouchPoint areas is not a group project. It is crucial that each member of your Diagnostic Review Board perform an individual evaluation to ensure the broadest spectrum of input. Each member will have a unique perspective, which is what will give you "eyes to see" the things that perhaps are causing moments of ***misery*** for some of your patients, or at best are keeping them from experiencing the moments of ***magic*** you desire to create. Once completed, the board will assemble to combine the findings into one master checklist.

Not all TouchPoints are created equally. You may find that there are significant areas of disagreement. This only serves to prove that different people have higher sensitivities to certain TouchPoints than do others. Let this motivate you to consider each area as important, but also keep in mind that how closely the font color on your business card matches your stationary is not as important to your patients as the cleanliness of your examining rooms.

TOUCHPOINTS 360° CHECKLIST

SEE 360°

(Iconic Elements)

These are all the visual or iconic elements your patients experience with every point of contact they have with your practice. From your print and TV advertising to the visual cues they get inside your four walls, you are either ***being*** the brand or ***breaching*** the brand. Look for ways to improve upon your See 360° elements and achieve consistency. What your patients see will either make them feel they've made a wise choice or an unwise choice.

Marketing: *Are all visual elements consistent with our strategy?*

Own words that match the SBM	*Poor*	*Fair*	*Good*	*Great*
Logo	*Poor*	*Fair*	*Good*	*Great*
Color	*Poor*	*Fair*	*Good*	*Great*
Font	*Poor*	*Fair*	*Good*	*Great*
TV	*Poor*	*Fair*	*Good*	*Great*
Newspaper	*Poor*	*Fair*	*Good*	*Great*
Billboards	*Poor*	*Fair*	*Good*	*Great*
Website	*Poor*	*Fair*	*Good*	*Great*

Search Engine Optimization	*Poor*	*Fair*	*Good*	*Great*
Logos on Invoices	*Poor*	*Fair*	*Good*	*Great*
Brochures	*Poor*	*Fair*	*Good*	*Great*
Business Cards	*Poor*	*Fair*	*Good*	*Great*
Banners/Signs	*Poor*	*Fair*	*Good*	*Great*
Social Networking Sites	*Poor*	*Fair*	*Good*	*Great*

Performance: *Visually are all elements clean, organized, and aesthetically pleasing? Do our visual first impressions help or hurt the brand?*

Curb Appeal	*Poor*	*Fair*	*Good*	*Great*
Waiting Room	*Poor*	*Fair*	*Good*	*Great*
Treatment/ Examining Rooms	*Poor*	*Fair*	*Good*	*Great*
Reception Area	*Poor*	*Fair*	*Good*	*Great*
Appearance & Dress Code	*Poor*	*Fair*	*Good*	*Great*
White Glove Test (cleanliness)	*Poor*	*Fair*	*Good*	*Great*

Equipment (clean/functional)	*Poor*	*Fair*	*Good*	*Great*
Bathrooms (clean/functional)	*Poor*	*Fair*	*Good*	*Great*
Lighting	*Poor*	*Fair*	*Good*	*Great*

SOUND 360°

(Echoic Elements)

Is your sound consistent in both voice and music in your advertising? The voice that is used for electronic media is your "audio logo." Additionally, the sounds within your practice will affect your brand either positively or negatively. From the greeting at the door to the background music, your brand is being ***communicated*** or ***contradicted.*** Enhance your Sound 360° by narrating your service to patients; they aren't always aware how they are being served. (i.e. "I'll just adjust that pillow to make you more comfortable" ... or ... "Let me hold your jacket for you.")

Marketing: *Are our words consistent with our Strategy? Do our sound elements connect or confuse?*

Do our words match our Strategy?	*Poor*	*Fair*	*Good*	*Great*
Music	*Poor*	*Fair*	*Good*	*Great*
Audio Logo (same voice)	*Poor*	*Fair*	*Good*	*Great*

Website Audio (consistent)	*Poor*	*Fair*	*Good*	*Great*
Social Networking (same words)	*Poor*	*Fair*	*Good*	*Great*
E-speeches (24/7)	*Poor*	*Fair*	*Good*	*Great*

Performance: *Do ancillary sound elements enhance or detract from our brand? Do words and tone of staff match our brand promise?*

In-office Sounds (music, ambient)	*Poor*	*Fair*	*Good*	*Great*
How the Phone is answered	*Poor*	*Fair*	*Good*	*Great*
Greeting at Reception	*Poor*	*Fair*	*Good*	*Great*
Narrating Benefits & Services	*Poor*	*Fair*	*Good*	*Great*

TOUCH 360°
(Emotional Connections)

These are all the ways you "touch" your patients emotionally. When you tell them a compelling story in your advertising, or when you go the extra mile to help them with a need, you are making an emotional connection that produces loyalty. Is everyone on your staff focused on "WOWing" your patients or just getting through the day? Empower your staff to perform "WOW" moments and to practice prompt and attentive recovery whenever an unmet expectation occurs.

Marketing: *Do our patients' experiences match our brand's promise? Does our marketing connect people to our brand?*

Patient Experience matches Promise	*Poor*	*Fair*	*Good*	*Great*
Community Image – Giving Back	*Poor*	*Fair*	*Good*	*Great*
Bricks (stories) Connect Emotionally	*Poor*	*Fair*	*Good*	*Great*

Performance: *Are we delivering on the brand promise in our day to day dealings with patients?*

Wait Time	*Poor*	*Fair*	*Good*	*Great*
Human Touch/ Everyone Smiles	*Poor*	*Fair*	*Good*	*Great*
Know Patients' Names	*Poor*	*Fair*	*Good*	*Great*
Thank You's	*Poor*	*Fair*	*Good*	*Great*
Extra Mile	*Poor*	*Fair*	*Good*	*Great*

Helpful / Sincere	*Poor*	*Fair*	*Good*	*Great*
Connections (make it personal)	*Poor*	*Fair*	*Good*	*Great*
Considering Privacy	*Poor*	*Fair*	*Good*	*Great*
Recovery Policy	*Poor*	*Fair*	*Good*	*Great*
Moments of Magic	*Poor*	*Fair*	*Good*	*Great*
Ask for Feedback	*Poor*	*Fair*	*Good*	*Great*

The Neck-Up Check-Up

It's your practice, so set the example. It's time for you to take an honest assessment of your most important branding tool … you. You define the values and goals and you set the tone by delivering on your brand's promise through your actions. Your example and vigilance is crucial for success.

I also recommend that each staff member do an evaluation of themselves.

Respectful of Patients' Time	*Poor*	*Fair*	*Good*	*Great*
Caring/Thoughtful	*Poor*	*Fair*	*Good*	*Great*
Thorough	*Poor*	*Fair*	*Good*	*Great*

Personal	*Poor*	*Fair*	*Good*	*Great*
Compassionate	*Poor*	*Fair*	*Good*	*Great*
Listening	*Poor*	*Fair*	*Good*	*Great*

A downloadable PDF version of this TouchPoints 360° Checklist can be found at* **www.brandsformation.com

When each member of your Diagnostic Review Board has completed the TouchPoints 360° Checklist, it's time to meet and coordinate a master checklist. From here you will work together to brainstorm and problem solve so that you can be on a critical path to improving the overall health of your practice.

Critical Path Timeline

A critical path timeline will serve as a tool of accountability. This is just a fancy way to say, get a notepad and make a list of what needs to be done, then decide who will be responsible for doing it and what the deadline for getting it done will be. As obvious as this seems, creating such a timeline directs your staff regarding specific tasks and provides a checklist and timeline for getting them accomplished. Recall how patients are judging you on things that have little or nothing to do with your credentials or the outcome of their treatment. Addressing these items may seem mundane, but you are being judged on them. The critical path timeline you create gets these items off your plate but keeps them from being ignored. Again, everyone on your staff must "buy in" and be the brand.

I recommend you develop a regular process for acquiring feedback from your patients. This can simplify your maintenance and review of your TouchPoints 360° Checklist and give you valuable input on areas that require your attention. It will also serve as its very own TouchPoint as it will say to your patients, "I'm listening and I care."

After I had a very unsatisfactory experience with an X-ray technician, my referring doctor developed an evaluation form for all future patients to carry with them on any referral visits he ordered. This gave him instant feedback on how his patients were being treated and said to the other providers that he has a choice in which providers he refers. It not only serves to remind others to try harder, it also suggests *he* tries harder.

Be the first to know what your patients need. They may not even know themselves. So:

- Ask them about their experiences (good or bad) with your practice.

- Look for new ways to super serve their needs.

- Communicate your DM to them frequently – not just through your advertising, but to your most captive audience ... your current patients.

- Match the benefits you provide with the benefits they need.

- Revisit your checklist frequently and keep improving.

That was the most comprehensive part of the implementation process. You already understand the concepts of the following areas of implementation from Chapter 5 (Strategy) and Chapter 6 (Strategy Based Message.) However, for the sake of implementation I want to lay out a few specific steps for you to take.

STRATEGY

You may remember me saying that strategy is the most important part of the BrandsFormation® process. Where branding is concerned, everything hinges on this crucial aspect of implementation. Strategy is your long-term plan of action that is designed to help you succeed. It requires an extensive look at what your competition is doing and what they are not doing. So roll up your sleeves and get to work on the following:

- Have everyone on your staff read this book.

- Consider your competition. What are they claiming, where is there a void? What can you claim that others can't.

- Remember to take on the patient perspective. Brainstorm with your staff and ask some of your trusted patients to weigh in.

- Discuss ideas about what your Difference Maker should be. What is unique or better about your practice? What idea can you own? DECIDE.

- Your strategy should be easy to understand and easy to communicate.

- Create a plan for how you will get the word out. This will require consideration of who you want to reach, understanding of the advertising options available and how the human mind works, plus knowledge of where to get the best bang for your buck (see Chapters 7/Consistency and 8/Dominant Frequency.)

STRATEGY BASED MESSAGE

Your strategy based message tells your DM in a clear and impactful way. The goal is to own a word or set of words that clearly communicate who you are and why I should choose you. What's your Difference Maker? Tell it to me here! (i.e. Crest: their long-term strategy or DM was cavity prevention ... their SBM was "Look Ma, no cavities!")

- Remember that words matter.

- Consider the mortar elements (voice, music, words you want to own.)

- Brainstorm the Bricks (the stories) that help dramatize your DM (chapter 6/Strategy Based Message) Mortar is static. Bricks are fluid. You will want to change your Bricks (stories) about every 6 weeks.

- Refer to the sample ads in Chapter 6/Strategy Based Message, which demonstrate bricks and mortar. Use this as a template to design your own strategy based message (mortar) and add the drama to your difference maker with your stories (bricks.)

As the old saying goes:

You never get a second chance to make a first impression.

It's true! Each of the patient stories at the opening of this chapter are real. Do any of your patients have similar stories to tell about you? OR ... have you created stories that are consistent with your brand promise? Are you taking steps to see that similar stories aren't being shared about your practice? BrandsFormation® will help you take control of how people feel about you and what they say about you.

By following each of these crucial steps, you are well on your way to being the healthcare practice people think of first.

On a Personal Note

"The difference between a successful person and others is not a lack of strength, not a lack of knowledge, but rather a lack of will."

This quote comes from a great Italian philosopher named Vince Lombardi, who also happened to coach the World Champion Green Bay Packers. If you're just starting a new healthcare practice, you don't need to go out looking for the "will" to be successful. That comes pretty naturally in the form of bank debt and maybe even a family to support. For those of you with older, more established healthcare practices, I think Vince is encouraging you to have the "guts to leave the ruts" and not keep the status quo.

Many of you may feel gung ho about what you've read and come out of the gate really enthusiastic, only to tire in the first lap and give up. Several of you may even set this book aside and it become nothing more than a dust catcher for your cleaning crew to swipe over. But some of you, are going to take all I've said to heart, put my methods to work and transform, excuse me, BrandsForm® your practice to a point of success you never imagined was possible. Those of you who don't use what I've taught are not necessarily destined for failure or even mediocrity. It's possible, I'm sure, to find great marketing success another way. I don't have those playbooks. I just have this one, and

I know it works. So if you implement BrandsFormation®, and I hope you do, you'll find the rewards I've witnessed over and over again with each of my clients. I may never hear about your success, but I'd love to.

As you have made it your life's work to help people and hopefully make their lives better, it is my desire to make business owners' marketing efforts pay off and increase their business. Patients often live under the circumstances of nagging pain, chronic illness and undiagnosed health issues. You have the ability to help people overcome, not just manage those problems. I hope you see the similarities.

I want you to overcome what burdens most healthcare professionals ... the business of doing business. It's my prescription for you and your practice to not only get better...but to experience continued growth and prosperity for years to come.

Indeed, the best is yet to come.

Endnotes

1. Jack Trout. Trout on Strategy. New York: McGraw-Hill, 2004,13-29.

2. Leonard L. Berry and Kent D. Seltman. Management Lessons from Mayo Clinic. New York: McGraw-Hill, 2008, 169.

3. Fred Lee. If Disney Ran Your Hospital. Second River Healthcare Press. 2004, 10.

4. BJ Bueno. Video-taped Interview. The Cult Branding Company.

5. Design for Services. Harvard Business Review on Touchpoints Term. http://designforservice.wordpress.com/2007/11/07/on-the-origin-of-touchpoints/ (Sept 14, 2010).